Becoming a Therapy Dog Team:

Guidance and Advice

By

Katha Miller-Winder, Ph.d.

Contents

Introduction

So you want to do Therapy Dog work; good for you! You've just told me something important. You've told me that you and your dog care about others and want them to feel valued and loved. You've told me that together with your dog you want to make people feel less alone. You want people to smile and laugh and feel like they matter. The love a dog shares does all of that. Therapy Dog teams make the world a better place; the world needs more of them.

I hear from lots of people who think they might like to do Therapy Dog work but they have no idea what's involved, how to get started, or what to expect. When I first realized my newly adopted dog Ranger was born to do Therapy Dog work, I was in the same boat. At the time I was vaguely aware that Therapy Dogs existed but I had no idea exactly what they were or what I and my dog needed to know so he could be one. What I knew at that point was that my dog loved EVERYONE and that everyone was drawn to him. You know you've got an extra special dog on your hands when the neighbors see you walking down the street with him and come out to pet him, leaving their own barking dogs inside. I was determined to do right by my dog and make sure he'd live the best life he could doing what he most wanted to do—love everyone he met. I needed to figure out how to do that.

My solution was to go online and do some research. Prowling through the long list of Therapy Dog organizations, I discovered one that was headquartered about 90 minutes from where we live. I ordered their training book and Ranger and I began working through it. We practiced each exercise and studied all the rules. We carefully introduced Ranger to everyone we met in a wheelchair or using a walker. We spent time at playgrounds. I thought I was doing what I needed to do so that we'd be prepared for the test. We finished the book and concluded we were ready. I scheduled our test and we promptly failed.

A couple years passed. Ranger and I both got a little older and wiser. We kept training and I kept learning about Therapy Dog work. And all along I knew this is what my dog was born to do. I thought we were ready to try again but when I went back to the organization's website, I found that they'd changed their rules quite a bit. Reading through all the new rules, I became more and more uncomfortable with the militant way that the organization was declaring how things should be done. I recognize that rules are necessary, but I also realize that one size does not always fit all and that there needs to be some flexibility and room for people to use their best judgment. I didn't want to be part of an organization who expressed their rules as if there were no other valid points of view.[1]

I was just starting to research other Therapy Dog organizations when another well respected Therapy Dog organization offered a test in the very place we call home. I promptly signed us up. The rest, as they say, is history. We passed our test, joined the organization, and then bumped into the 'now what' problem. Fortunately for me the group that had sponsored the test had set up an informal visit at a nearby nursing home. So Ranger and I showed up to join the group visiting this nursing home. I had no idea what it would be like or how much the emotional toll would affect both of us as we interacted with people in serious mental and physical decline. It was clear that our visit was the highlight of the month for

---

[1] I'm pleased to note that they've softened their language in the intervening years.

the people we visited and we witnessed smiles and laughter from people who were emotionally shut down when we arrived. It was wonderful and terrible in equal measure but one thing was certain. We had made a big difference; we'd brought joy to people who needed it. When I witnessed all the smiles and the joy we brought with our visit, I was hooked.

What you hold in your hands is the book I wish I'd had all those years ago when I began this journey. It's all the tips and tricks I've learned along the way with the guidance and advice I wish I'd had in the beginning. This book will help you understand the realities of Therapy Dog work, what skills are needed, things to consider, and how to get started. It's the basic information and tools you need backed up by research and experience and wrapped in personal anecdotes that will help to illustrate specific points.

If you're ready to become a Therapy Dog team but are hesitant to dive into the unknown and just want someone to be there to guide you along the way, this book is for you. If you've always been a little curious what Therapy Dog work was all about and why people do it, this book is for you. If you're a trainer, veterinarian, groomer, or other dog professional who has people asking them about Therapy Dog work but you've had no idea how to help them find answers, this book is for you. However, if you're looking for detailed instructions about how to train your dog for Therapy Dog work there are force-free rewards-based dog training books out there that will serve you better. In this book we will cover the skills a Therapy Dog needs and we'll discuss the foundations upon which I've built the specific cue training I've done with my own dogs, but how to train the cues we use isn't part of this book.

Who Am I?

At this point it's probably helpful if I introduce myself, my dogs, and my qualifications. I got into Therapy Dog work because that was clearly what my first Therapy Dog, Ranger, was born to do. I'd grown up with dogs, cats, chickens, ducks, sheep, pigs, ponies, and even a steer, but Ranger was my first dog as an adult. I'd just completed breast cancer treatment and I wasn't going to postpone things I wanted anymore. I'd wanted a dog of my own for a long time so I announced to my husband and children that we were getting a dog. A few days I later loaded my 14-

year-old and 8-year-old children into the car and went to the Humane Society. Since the last pet we'd adopted was a new kitten and it had taken nearly six months to find the right one to join our household, I didn't expect to find the perfect dog on our first visit but there he was. According to his adoption paperwork, Ranger was a one-year-old Border Collie mix who had been surrendered due to a death in his previous family. It was obvious immediately that Ranger had been greatly loved and had received fabulous socialization. What became obvious very quickly is that Ranger had received basically no training. No one in their right mind would bring home a high energy herding mix with no training mere weeks after completing cancer treatment but no one said I was in my right mind—cancer treatment will do that to you.

In his career Ranger documented more than 500 visits. We weren't keeping track in the beginning so I'm not sure how many visits he totaled over all. We visited nursing homes, memory care units, long-term care facilities, retirement communities, schools, colleges, and libraries. He became a registered Therapy Dog when he was four years old and retired about a month before we had to let him go; he was nearing 13 and had an aggressive form of cancer.

My current Therapy Dog is a Great Pyrenees named D'Artagnan. He received his official credentials allowing him to visit just in time for in-person visits to be canceled due to the COVID-19 pandemic. Together D'Artagnan and I have learned to think outside traditional in-person Therapy Dog work and find ways to still make a positive difference in the lives of people. The things we've learned are examined in the chapter about visiting.

I've been a Therapy Dog handler/partner for about a decade now. I serve as a local director for a well respected Therapy Dog organization and recently became an evaluator for the organization. Because reputable Therapy Dog organizations are non-profits, I won't be naming the organization to which I belong. Doing so would potentially be profiting from my association with them, which is ethically wrong.

People who do Therapy Dog work should adhere to the highest ethical standards. As a visiting Therapy Dog team you'll be there as a volunteer and you should not profit from or charge for your visits. In purchasing this book you are buying access to my knowledge and experience. This book is not affiliated with or authorized by any Therapy Dog organization. My knowledge and experience are mine to do with as I like, provided I adhere to the rules and standards governing the things I learn about the people I visit.

As a Therapy Dog team you must comply with HIPAA (Health Insurance Portability and Accountability Act) standards. HIPAA prohibits sharing health information about residents except to those the resident or guardian has specifically designated. As you visit you may learn things about a patient's condition but no matter how tempting it might be to share that information with someone else, as a Therapy Dog team you are also bound by HIPAA rules. In this book I take pains to avoid any identifying details, including gender, that might reveal who I am talking about when I share relevant stories about visits I've made with my dogs. This is part of the responsibility a Therapy Dog team has to care for the well-being and privacy of the people you visit. This responsibility includes a duty to report any abuse you may witness or suspect to the appropriate authorities. States have a responsibility to make it easy to find the appropriate place to report abuse. Most states do this by posting numbers to report abuse throughout the facilities.

The other important ethical consideration is your duty to care for and respect your dog. You should never force your dog to visit or push your dog beyond their willing cooperation. You are first and foremost responsible for the wellbeing and comfort of your dog. I'm a lifelong learner. I love to learn about things that interest me, and dogs and Therapy Dog work are no different. In order to be the best possible partner for my Therapy Dogs I want a thorough understanding of canine body language, dog behaviorism, and current scientific research on dog behavior and training. The more I know, the better I can support the well-being and comfort of my canine partner.

I have encouraged, supported, observed, and mentored a lot of Therapy Dog teams over the years. In my observation there are two types of successful teams. The first is teams in which the dog was clearly born to do Therapy Dog work and would happily choose the job if it was solely within their power. The second type of successful team is where the human partner is the one that has a passion for the work, and the dog is happy to cooperate because they get to do it with their person. The truly exceptional teams are those where the human has a passion for the work and the dog was born for the job. But it doesn't matter whether you, your dog, or both of you have a passion for the job: it's a job worth doing and one that makes a tremendous positive difference in the world.

How to Use this Book

One book cannot answer every question but this book should provide a good solid foundation for understanding what Therapy Dog work is like and the skills you and your dog will need. It should provide a sense of what things you want to look for when choosing an organization to join and how to decide which of the many factors are really important to you. In the pages that follow you'll discover what a visit is like and why you never know what to expect. You'll read heartwarming stories and learn the tips and tricks I teach Therapy Dog teams I mentor in person.

There is a lot to learn about Therapy Dog work. Some of it is obvious but there are also a lot of subtle and nuanced things to learn. In this book I've tried to illustrate both. If you're just getting your bearings in Therapy Dog work, the format of the book should take you through all the things to consider and answer your questions. If you have specific questions you should be able to find the answer in the relevant chapter or by using the index. I live in the United States and the book is written from a US perspective; however, much of the information should be broadly applicable everywhere Therapy Dog programs exist.

No matter how you choose to use this book you ought to find it helpful. It should help you navigate the different factors involved in Therapy Dog work and guide you to the confidence you need to get started.

Chapter One: What Is a Therapy Dog— Untangling Definitions

Dogs work in our society in many different ways and each job has its own label. These labels can create confusion as they are misapplied and misused. Misconceptions about how the law applies to different types of assistive dog jobs also create confusion. In this chapter we will look at three of the most commonly misused and misunderstood labels. We'll look briefly at the training each type of assistive dog needs, who the dog is trained to work with, where the dog is able to go, and the nature of their work environment. The three types of assistive working dogs are Service Dogs, including Psychological Service Dogs, Emotional Support Dogs, and Therapy Dogs. The label Therapy Dog is perhaps the least understood. Let's take a look at what a Therapy Dog is and what it is not. A Therapy Dog is not a Service Dog or an Emotional Support Dog.

I'm often contacted by people who want my help in finding or training a dog that will provide them with emotional support and/or help alleviate a mental health condition. When that happens I gently explain that a Therapy Dog is not a personal dog providing emotional support and helping to ease psychological conditions. Dogs that do those jobs are Emotional Support Dogs or Psychological Service Dogs. Which one of those two labels is appropriate depends on the specific role the dog fulfills. Psychological Service Dogs are employed to manage a mental health condition and trained to perform specific tasks in relation to that condition. Emotional Support Dogs are employed in a more general supportive role where the love they give their handler makes the handler feel more grounded and able to cope. While these dogs are necessary and wonderful, they are not the subject of this book.

Service Dogs

But we should start at the beginning by looking at the legal definition for the different types of assistance dogs. The best known of these helper dogs is a Service Dog. Service Dogs are considered medical equipment; just as you are allowed to use your wheelchair or oxygen tank in any public space, you are allowed to use your Service Dog in any public space.

According to the Americans with Disabilities Act,

> Service animals are defined as dogs that are individually trained to do work or perform tasks for people with disabilities. Examples of such work or tasks include guiding people who are blind, alerting people who are deaf, pulling a wheelchair, alerting and protecting a person who is having a seizure, reminding a person with mental illness to take prescribed medications, calming a person with Post Traumatic Stress Disorder (PTSD) during an anxiety attack, or performing other duties. Service animals are working animals, not pets. The work or task a dog has been trained to provide must be directly related to the person's disability. Dogs whose sole function is to provide comfort or emotional support do not qualify as service animals under the ADA.[2]

---

[2] **Service Animals** ADA 2010 Revised Requirements: Service Animals

In other words, Service Dogs are specially trained to perform helpful tasks for their medically compromised partner. The most familiar Service Dog is probably a Guide Dog for a blind person. Guide Dogs act as eyes to help the blind person navigate the world. However, as the quote makes clear, Service Dogs are trained to perform a multitude of other tasks. These run the gamut from smelling a diabetic's insulin needs to fetching and carrying for a mobility challenged partner. Service dogs are also trained to bring their partner's medications, to press buttons to summon help, to alert a deaf person to important sounds, and to perform many, many more invaluable assistive tasks. Service Dogs are amazing and they are life changing for their partners.

Psychological Service Dogs are a subset of Service Dogs. Perhaps the best known role for this type of Service Dog is supporting a person with PTSD (Post Traumatic Stress Disorder). Dogs serving in this role are trained for such tasks as entering dark rooms and turning on the lights. They can also get their partner safely out of a busy public space such as a mall during a PTSD episode, and they stand between their partner and other people as a physical barrier to help their partner to feel safe. Just like any Service Dog, Psychological Service Dogs are medical equipment and can go anywhere in public.

Emotional Support Dogs

Emotional Support Dogs are part of the category Emotional Support Animals. Michigan State University's Animal Legal and Historical Center defines them as follows:

> An emotional support animal is an animal (typically a dog or cat though this can include other species) that provides a therapeutic benefit to its owner through companionship. The animal provides emotional support and comfort to individuals with psychiatric disabilities and other mental impairments. The animal is not specifically trained to perform tasks for a person who suffers from emotional disabilities. Unlike a service animal, an emotional support animal is not granted access to places of public accommodation. Under the federal Fair Housing Act (FHA), an emotional support animal is viewed as a "reasonable accommodation" in a

housing unit that has a "no pets" rule for its residents.[3]

Emotional Support Dogs require no special training and have only one right not granted to any pet dog. Emotional Support Dogs can live in housing where pets are prohibited. A person who is reliant on a pet for emotional support and comfort can obtain a letter from a physician confirming that they have a mental or physical disability that is mitigated by their Emotional Support Dog. That letter requires the landlord to make the reasonable accommodation of allowing the dog to live there. In all other respects an Emotional Support Dog is indistinguishable from a pet dog. Some Emotional Support Dogs may be highly trained canine companions with impeccable manners while others may be essentially untrained friendly dogs.

Therapy Dogs

Both Emotional Support Dogs and Service Dogs are expected to work with an individual person. Therapy Dogs are different; their job is to engage with multiple people.

---

[3] **FAQs on Emotional Support Animals** Animal Law Legal Center

Therapy Dogs do not have the same rights of public access as Service Dogs but they are allowed anywhere they are invited.[4] Therapy Dogs are frequently invited to visit hospitals, memory care units, nursing homes, rehab centers, schools, libraries, and more. Some of these places will have pet friendly policies that allow visits by friendly pets. This leads to the question: how is a Therapy Dog different than simply a visiting pet? The biggest difference is that Therapy Dogs are specifically trained to engage with a wide variety of people and have been independently evaluated for visiting suitability by a Therapy Dog organization. They are registered or certified by recognized Therapy Dog organizations that provide them with a liability insurance policy held by the organization. These dogs are more than simply friendly pets; they are working dogs doing a specialized visiting job.

---

[4] "Definition of a Service Dog vs. Emotional Support Animal vs. Therapy Dog."

Animal Assisted Therapy

Therapy Dogs do two types of work: Animal Assisted Therapy (AAT) and Animal Assisted Activity (AAA). AAT is a dog working under the supervision of a medical professional to achieve treatment plan goals. Examples of this include a dog working with a physical therapist fetching a ball when thrown by the client or a dog cuddling a client in a psychologist's office during a session. There is considerable overlap between a dog doing AAA and one doing AAT. As a result it is not uncommon for a mental health professional using their dog in their practice to train, test, and register their dog with a Therapy Dog organization. Doing this provides an independent evaluation of the suitability of the dog for Therapy Dog work and serves as confirmation for the medical professional's insurance provider that the dog won't significantly increase the liability risk of the practice. A Therapy Dog, registered with an organization, isn't covered by the organization's volunteer liability insurance if the dog is being used at their handler/partner's job. AAT is an invaluable service but because it requires close coordination with a medical professional, it's outside the scope of this book. In this book we'll focus on AAA.

Animal Assisted Activities

So what is Animal Assisted Activity exactly? The term is a little amorphous. Therapy Dog organization Angel Paws provides this definition,

> Animal Assisted Activities (AAA) provide opportunities for recreational, motivational, educational, &/or [sic] therapeutic benefits to aid healing, speed recovery and enhance quality of life. AAA are delivered by specifically trained volunteers in association with animals that meet specific criteria.[5]

In other words AAA is when trained and independently evaluated teams are used to help people feel better. Therapy Animals: Animals Helping People defines AAA as "the use of animals in recreational and visitation programs to help people with special needs..."[6] In the simplest terms AAA happens when interaction with the dog makes the recipient feel better. This can happen when someone

---

[5] "WHAT IS Animal Assisted Activities & Therapy (AAA/T)?" *Therapy Dogs Ohio | Animal Assisted Therapy Columbus Ohio | Angel Paws*
[6] "What Is AAT/AAA?" *Therapy Animals*

is petting the dog, watching the dog do tricks, or sharing stories about dogs they have loved while a visiting dog is in the room. In short, any interaction between a person being visited and a Therapy Dog is AAA unless the interaction has a defined therapeutic goal overseen by a medical professional.

Benefits of Animal Assisted Activities

An ever growing body of scientific evidence shows that petting a dog has health benefits. The abstract of a study conducted by Therapy Dogs International, Inc from 1996 to 1998 summarized it like this;

> Data indicated an overwhelming perception that patients benefited in a variety of ways, including increased socialization, verbalization, alertness, and positive mood alterations. Staff were reported to benefit by increased morale, using dog visits as a break in their work, and being able to observe patients interacting with the dogs.[7]

[7] Jones, Jacqueline. "Perceptions of the Impact of Pet Therapy on Residents/Patients and Staff in Facilities Visited by Therapy Dogs." *Therapy Dogs International*

This study relied heavily on observational reports. More recent studies have worked to confirm these observations with quantifiable scientific research.

UCLA Health Animal Assisted Therapy Research compiled the following list of health benefits that come from petting and interacting with a dog.

For Mental Health:

- The simple act of petting animals releases an automatic relaxation response.
  - Humans interacting with animals have found that petting the animal promoted the release of serotonin, prolactin and oxytocin- all hormones that can play a part in elevating moods.
- Lowers anxiety and helps people relax.
- Provides comfort.
- Reduces loneliness.
- Increases mental stimulation.
  - Assist in recall of memories and help sequence temporal events in patients with head injuries or chronic diseases

such as Alzheimer's disease.

- Can provide an escape or happy distraction.
- Can act as catalysts in the therapy process.
    - May help break the ice.
    - May reduce the initial resistance that might accompany therapy.

For Physical Health:

- Lowers blood pressure and improves cardiovascular health.
- Reduces the amount of medications some people need.
- Breathing slows in those who are anxious.
- Releases many hormones such as Phenylethylamine which has the same effect as chocolate.
- Diminishes overall physical pain.
- Relax more during exercise.
    - Participants were motivated, enjoyed the therapy sessions more, and felt the atmosphere of the session was less stressful during Animal-Assisted therapy.

- For Children with Autism
  - Many children with autism feel a deep bond with animals and feel that they are able to relate better than humans.
  - Children with autism were engaged in significantly greater use of language as well as social interaction win their therapy sessions that incorporated animals compared to standard therapy sessions without them.[8]

These two studies are just a small sample of the research detailing the tremendous benefits Therapy Dogs provide. I cited these in order to illustrate that the earlier research efforts relied mostly on somewhat subjective observation and more recent research efforts measure the physiological effects of Therapy Dog interaction.

---

[8] "Animal-Assisted Therapy Research." *UCLA People-Animal Connection*

Animal Assisted Activities in Action

In my own Therapy Dog work I've seen firsthand some of the amazing things Therapy Dogs accomplish. In this section I will share some of the effects of AAA I've witnessed from the different places my Therapy Dogs and I have visited over the years.

On one visit early in our career Ranger and I got to observe firsthand the physiological effects of petting a dog. This visit came when the effects on blood pressure of petting a dog were first becoming widely known. One resident had just received a blood-pressure reading that was bordering on dangerously high. I was asked to bring my dog over to the resident and let them interact for a minute. After that minute, a second blood pressure check was done and this time the reading was well within normal limits. After petting and interacting with my dog for just one minute, this resident's blood pressure went from being worryingly high to being within the normal range. The staff and I all got to see, as science had already found, the effect that petting and loving a dog has on blood pressure.

I've also seen firsthand the effect a dog can have on a dementia patient. We were visiting the memory care unit of a long-term care facility and Ranger led me immediately to a patient sitting alone with arms crossed. The patient looked at Ranger and I could see the failed effort to reach for Ranger to pet him. At that moment the circuits controlling arm muscle movement weren't functioning for this individual, and I could see the panic on the face of the resident beginning as something as familiar as moving arms was blocked. Ranger, a very experienced and intuitive Therapy Dog by this point, without any prompting from me, settled himself on the floor. I knew to trust that he knew what he was doing and this time was no exception. His changing position was enough to unlock the resident's muscle circuits and the patient leaned over to pet him. After a few minutes the patient was smiling, focused, engaged, and present in the moment. We were visiting as part of a group and each dog visited with this patient in succession. By the time we left the area the patient was laughing out loud and demonstrating fluid movements.

With Ranger I participated in afterschool programs where students were able to read to him. He was incredibly popular with the kids. This program was for at-risk students and there were occasions of acting out. One student had outbursts of rage that could include throwing chairs. One day when we could all see the student building up to an outburst, Ranger got up from where he was waiting for the next reader. Since we were connected by his leash and I'd learned I could safely trust his instincts, I followed to see what he planned to do. Ranger walked over and sat down just out of reach of the student. All he did was sit in the general area of the student, but I saw the rage draining away and the student relax. When this happened Ranger stood and walked to the student, nudging at the hand to demand petting. After a few seconds of this Ranger took me back so he could listen to another story. In a very short time he had altered the student's mood dramatically.

When visiting a care facility sometimes you are asked to visit a resident or patient that has entirely withdrawn. Staff will tell you they haven't spoken in weeks or even months. You'll walk into the room with your dog wondering what difference your visit could make, but this is where amazing things happen. While doing Therapy Dog work with Ranger I learned to expect the miraculous. We'd walk into the room and find the resident in bed. Ranger would approach the bed and as I'd call out, "Would you like a visit from a dog?" Ranger would slide his nose under a hand. He'd remain with his nose in the hand, maybe nudging it a bit while I would introduce Ranger and talk about how he loved visiting people and being petted. I'd watch the fingers begin to move and a few tentative pats happen. "Do you like dogs?" I'd ask, and a rusty disused voice would weakly reply, "Yes." When we were visiting in a group, after Ranger another dog would come in and by the time all of the dogs had visited, the resident could be sitting on the edge of the bed asking questions and talking about the various dogs. This is the effect Therapy Dogs have. AAA may not sound very exciting but the effects can be incredible.

Chapter Two: Specialized Therapy Dogs

Three more AAA roles merit discussion. These are listening to kids read stories, reducing stress for those working disaster sites, and dogs working in courtrooms. Therapy Dog is a name employed pretty consistently but there isn't a consistent name for dogs that listen to stories, dogs that provide comfort and support at disasters, and dogs that work in courtrooms. We'll look at each of these roles in turn.

Reading to a Dog

Dogs that listen to readers are variously called Tail Waggin' Tutors (Therapy Dogs International), Reading Education Assistance Dogs READ (Pet Partners), and many other terms. These dogs can be found in schools and libraries listening to kids read to them. Reading to a dog has been shown to boost reading scores.

A group of third grade students from both an elementary school and a homeschool situation participated in a ten-week research study by the University of California Davis Veterinary Medicine Extension in 2010. Students read to a dog once a week for about 15 minutes after simply sitting with the dog for a few minutes. Their reading fluency was evaluated using the Oral Text Reading for Comprehension test at the beginning and end of the ten-week session. Readers in the school setting improved their fluency by 12%, while the control students did not increase their fluency at all over the same time period. The home-schooled readers increased their fluency by 30%.

> Qualitatively, the participants in the program believed it was a huge success. Before the program started, many of the young readers didn't feel good about reading aloud. Afterwards, they felt more confident in their reading skills and also felt safe when reading to a dog. Their opinions of reading changed from feeling uncomfortable and self-conscience (sic) before the program to

proclaiming that reading was much more enjoyable for them now.[9]

My husband got an unexpected demonstration of just how powerful reading to a dog can be one evening as he was walking Ranger around our neighborhood. Ranger and I had been listening to stories at a district-wide summer school program for struggling readers. As my husband was walking the dog, a trio of kids on bicycles stopped to see if they could pet Ranger. This was a very common occurrence so my husband didn't think anything of it; Ranger was always happy to soak up a little more attention. As the kids were petting Ranger, one of them commented about how he was like the dog named Ranger they read to at summer school. When my husband replied that it was Ranger, the delighted kid redoubled the attention to Ranger while telling the friends that they should come to summer school as well so they could read to Ranger. Being forced to go to summer school is generally regarded as something unpleasant but getting to read to dogs had turned it into something so positive that a student was telling friends that they were missing out by not going.

---

[9] "Reading to Dogs: A Library's Guide to Getting Started." *Research - Reading to Dogs: A Library's Guide to Getting Started.*

Ranger was a genius at listening to kids read. He figured out that the voice cadence of a person reading and a person talking is different. After a few times of hearing me gently redirect the child back to reading, he decided he'd do it himself. When a child began to chatter instead of read, he'd take his great big paw and smack it down on the book. I'd explain that Ranger was saying he wanted to hear the story and the child would immediately go back to reading. They generally stayed pretty well focused on reading after Ranger told them he wanted to hear the story. Often Ranger would fall sound asleep when listening to readers. I always gave that a positive spin, telling them it was a great accomplishment reading him to sleep and to keep reading so he'd stay asleep. I'd emphasize that they were doing a great job.

The best thing about reading to a dog is how non-judgmental dogs are. The dog doesn't care if you're a fluid reader or only able to read the illustrations. A dog is happy to curl up next to you and just be there. Unlike a person a dog doesn't try to help when you don't need it or offer unwanted suggestions; a dog just lets you get on with it as best you can. During our time with the afterschool program for at-risk kids we got to watch one reluctant third grade reader go from barely being able to read a simple Bob book ("This is Bob. He has a job." is the level of text) to reading chapter books to Ranger.

Comfort After a Disaster

There are also dogs that go into disaster and crisis situations. These dogs go by such names as Crisis Response Dogs, Comfort Dogs, and Disaster Stress Relief Dogs, to name a few.

Disaster Stress Relief Dogs have been filling a recognized role since 1995. That's when Therapy Dogs International first identified the need for Therapy Dogs trained to the highest level to serve in the aftermath of a crisis or disaster.

> Therapy Dogs International began their Disaster Stress Relief Dogs program after the Oklahoma City bombing. "Approximately 20 Therapy Dogs International volunteers and their dogs responded after the bombing of the Murrah Federal building in Oklahoma City in 1995. This was our first experience in working with people affected by a terrorist attack. The emotional impact

of the attack affected most people in the United States. To remember the victims and the helpers at the Oklahoma City bombing, we created a special newsletter in the fall of 1995 *Heartache in the Heartland.* Here is a quote from this newsletter, a quote that can be applied to any disaster where we have responded.

"...Dogs were hugged and petted by the families of the victims, displaced persons, members of the Red Cross and the Salvation Army, clergy, police officers, firefighters, U.S. Army Reserve troops and other relief workers."[10]

After the terrorist attack on the Twin Towers in New York the importance of these furry therapists became widely recognized.

Disaster relief dogs, also called crisis response dogs, gained recognition after the events of September 11, 2001, when they played an important role in helping survivors heal. In recent years, disaster relief dogs have comforted victims of shootings, mudslides, and hurricanes. These special dogs and their human

---

[10] "Oklahoma City Bombing, April 1995 Heartache in the Heartland." *Therapy Dogs International*

handlers alleviate trauma and help people heal.[11]

Therapy Dogs who are working crisis response at a disaster site do a lot of good simply by being there for people to love. However, Therapy Dog teams do more than merely share love.

> Therapy Dog volunteers are the key that unlocks the door through which professionals can enter the world of people affected by disasters. Because people are drawn to dogs, people will talk to a Therapy Dog handler, or, often, a Therapy Dog, when they are still in shock; when they are unable to process the necessary information available from professional assistance. Therapy Dog handlers perform a necessary triage service by assessing the needs of an individual and discreetly beckoning the appropriate health care worker to come to the aid of the individual, thus getting the right help to the right person at the right time.

> The Therapy Dogs also provide hugging time for the professionals (including police officers, firefighters, medical professionals and other relief

---

[11] Geier, Elisabeth. "The Astounding Heroics of Disaster Relief Dogs." *The Dog People by Rover.com*, 8 June 2018

workers and volunteers, as well as members of the clergy), who suffer their own emotional pain when dealing with the devastating pain of others.[12]

Dogs and handlers that go into disaster situations have a lot more training and expectations than the average Therapy Dog team. In addition to knowing which health care worker is best suited to the needs of the person they're comforting and discreetly summoning them, Therapy Dog handler/partners need to have a clear knowledge of the roles in disaster management, who has the authority to do what, and the recognized chains of command.

In a disaster situation there is a site manager who is responsible for all the personnel working at the site. This manager chooses which resources are required and invites those who are best suited to provide them. Unless they are invited, resources are not welcome at the site. This includes Therapy Dog teams. Several Therapy Dog organizations have teams that are specially qualified to serve at a disaster site. The site manager will invite teams from one or

---

[12] "Oklahoma City Bombing, April 1995 Heartache in the Heartland."

sometimes more organizations to provide comfort and support to those affected by the disaster and those working at the site. Not all Therapy Dog teams have the necessary temperament, knowledge, or skill to work in a crisis or disaster situation.

Following a natural disaster in our region where many people lost their lives, my partner Ranger and I were invited to interview to help in providing comfort to those affected. It turned out that there was a miscommunication; the person who had invited the organization we were with was not in fact the site manager. The actual site manager had chosen a different organization and didn't want to have two different organizations on site. Before we learned of this miscommunication, we went through the interview process.

The interview process was interesting. First, I met with a panel of people who asked me questions clearly designed to assess my mental and emotional ability to cope with the heavy burden of being around people who had lost everything. In the area affected situations arose where a search and rescue worker could be recovering dead family members. The interviewers were interested in finding out how those of us interviewing would deal with someone who had experienced that. They also wanted to know why we wanted to do this work. My response was to quote the Mr. Rogers' story where he talked about how his mother had told him that when bad things happen he should look for the helpers. I said that I wanted to be one of those helpers. I couldn't fix things for the search and rescue worker who'd just pulled a relative from the mud, but I could be there to let them know people cared and that they weren't alone and most of all to let my dog work his magic.

The second part of the interview focused on the dog. Ranger was asked to demonstrate strict obedience despite a wealth of distractions. When working a disaster site, a dog needs to be rock solid, to listen and obey instantly when the handler cues a behavior, and to be focused regardless of whatever else is going on around them. Ranger and I did very well on the focus and unflappable part of the interview, but I train my dogs to make good decisions rather than to be strictly obedient so we did not shine on that part; he refused to sit when asked. He willingly turned his back on the barking Doberman across the street and downed when asked but refused the sit cue. He was calm and under control at all times but not strictly obedient. He would have been allowed by the organization to work outside the boundaries of the disaster site but not within them.

Dogs at the Courthouse

The last of the specialized Therapy Dogs to discuss here are those that go into courtrooms and otherwise play a role in legal proceedings providing emotional support for victims and witnesses who are emotionally fragile. This is a complex area where both professional assistance dogs trained as Service Dogs and traditionally trained Therapy Dogs do much the same work. The professional Service Dogs in this case are asked to work with a variety of individuals like Therapy Dogs do. Dogs trained first as Service Dogs are referred to as Courthouse Facility Dogs.

> [A] courthouse facility dog is a professionally trained facility dog that has graduated from an accredited assistance dog organization that is a member of Assistance Dogs International. Such dogs assist crime victims, witnesses, and others during the investigation and prosecution of crimes, as well as

during other legal proceedings. Courthouse facility dogs also provide assistance to Drug Court and Mental Health Court and participants during their recovery from drugs, alcohol, mental illness and post traumatic stress disorder.[13]

While the number of Courthouse Facility Dogs is growing, the need still far outstrips their availability. Traditional Therapy Dogs are being asked to take on some of the same functions.

Animals, particularly dogs, are increasingly being integrated into court and related settings, most often in cases involving children. The dogs are intended to provide emotional support to victims who are involved in the many phases of legal proceedings. Two program models are most common. One approach requires that the dog's handler is a professional in the legal system. An alternate model relies on volunteer handler-animal teams. All programs require thorough training of both team members and attention at all times to the needs and cues of the animal.[14]

---

[13] "Courthouse Facility Dog."
[14] "Animals in Court and Related Settings"

Courthouse Facility Dogs only started being used regularly in the early 2000s so this is a relatively new purpose for dogs. As a result of the overlapping use of Courthouse Facility Dogs and traditional Therapy Dogs, rules aren't really standardized. It can be convoluted for a volunteer Therapy Dog team to figure out exactly what they are allowed to do. Each Therapy Dog organization that permits their teams to do courthouse work will have their own protocols which may vary widely. One organization may allow their dogs to work in the courtroom inside the witness box where another may only permit dogs registered with them to work in waiting areas.

The state of Alabama has clearly spelled out the importance, role, and expected behavior of a Therapy Dog team used in legal proceedings.

> (b) In a legal proceeding, to reduce the stress of the witness and to enhance the ability of the court to obtain full and accurate testimony, the court may allow a registered therapy dog to accompany a victim or witness while testifying, or in other court proceedings if a registered therapy dog is available.

(c) If the court, in its sole discretion, grants the use of a registered therapy dog, the registered therapy dog shall be accompanied by a registered handler who has received instruction from the district attorney's office on the protocols and policies of legal proceedings for that circuit and the role of the registered therapy dog and registered handler to assure there is no interference with the collection of evidence and testimony or the administration of justice.

(d) If a jury has been empaneled in the legal proceeding, the registered therapy dog shall be accompanied by the registered handler to the witness stand with the witness outside of the presence of the jury and the registered handler shall return to his or her position in the courtroom within view of the witness stand. Subsequently, the jury shall be seated and the court shall inform the jury of the presence of the registered therapy dog and instruct the jury that the presence of a registered therapy dog should not create any prejudice to any party.

(e) During trial proceedings all precautions should be taken to obscure the presence of a registered therapy dog from the jury.[15]

In situations where a Therapy Dog is used in the courtroom to support emotionally fragile witnesses or victims, the dog will be expected to work independently. In all other situations the dog will remain connected to the handler/partner by a leash. No matter where a Therapy Dog team serves in legal proceedings, the handler will need to have a solid understanding of legal protocol since indiscretion about anything heard in the course of the investigation or trial could taint the outcome.

Whether a Therapy Dog team is working in a courthouse, disaster site, or a school they are making a tremendous difference. The love and support of a dog makes everything better. Petting a dog is comforting and soothing and their mere presence is calming. Therapy Dogs are amazing.

---

[15] Statutes, Codes, and Regulations." *Legal Research Tools from Casetext*

Chapter Three: More than Petting—It's a Job

Many people don't think that Therapy Dog work requires actual effort on the part of the dog; after all, the dog is just getting love from people. People also think it's not really work for the handler/partner; after all, they're just walking their dog around so people can pet the dog. But this notion that it isn't work couldn't be further from the truth. Therapy Dog work takes tremendous effort, time, and emotional engagement for both halves of the team.

Dogs at Work

It's true that dogs love having us give them attention; they seek us out and solicit it. There's an important difference, though, between your dog seeking you out to ask for attention and petting and a Therapy Dog engaging with a number of different unknown people. Your dog already has a relationship with you but until the dog has visited a person several times, that person is still a stranger and the dog is being asked to make an instant connection with them.

Therapy Dogs are meeting a number of strangers every visit. When engaged in Therapy Dog work the dog is being asked to submit to petting by people they don't know who may have coordination challenges, arthritis so bad their hands are little more than clubs, or other physical challenges that cause them to pet the dog in an awkward and potentially unpleasant way. And the dog is asked to do this in a strange environment with people moving about in unpredictable ways, slippery floors, weird noises, and unpleasant smells. Products used to clean and disinfect facilities can be disagreeable to the human half of the team and even more so for the dogs.

As humans we often forget to consider scent and sound as problems for our dogs. Humans generally learn at a young age to simply tune out annoying sounds and smells. Our human senses of smell and of hearing are less acute than a dog's. The more acute senses of our dogs make it harder for them to tune out scents and sounds. In my Therapy Dog group we had one Therapy Dog that was obviously distressed at being in one of the facilities we visited.

This was strange because the other dogs enjoyed this favorite place to visit, and this dog was very happy to visit many similar facilities. It wasn't until her handler/partner had her in for her annual vet check that her specific facility dislike was understood. The facility the dog didn't like used the same cleaning products as her vet's office. The poor dog couldn't concentrate on visiting with people because she kept waiting for a vet to appear and subject her to the usual indignities. The facilities she was happy to visit may have used similar cleaning products but not the exact same ones.

When a Therapy Dog is working, they are focusing on the specific task of relating to a number of unfamiliar people. They are engaging with many people who want to pet them; people who generally aren't very good at listening or observing what the dog is saying about how they like to be petted. The majority of dogs don't care for having the tops of their heads stroked or patted. If you have a dog handy right now, invite them over for some petting. If you're like me, you may start with a stroke or two on the top but quickly shift to rubbing ears, the sides of the face, or under the chin. Those are the spots my dog loves to have me pet him, but not so much the top of his head.

On a Therapy Dog visit the dog is going to patiently endure a lot of the type of petting that they don't actually enjoy. They do this because it's what makes the person they're visiting feel good. As Therapy Dog handlers/partners part of our job is to encourage people to pet the dog in ways the dog enjoys and to explain gently why the dog shifts away from being petted in a way they do not enjoy.

Many of the people Ranger and I visited had physical challenges that rendered their petting more like thumping. Dogs don't like to be patted on the head and thumping is even more unpleasant. Ranger's solution was to shift until the thumping pats were happening between his shoulder blades. I'd smile and comment that Ranger liked them to pet him there on his shoulders and how he could always be counted on to get the kind of petting he liked best. They felt like they were doing nice things for him and he was being subjected to a much more tolerable form of petting. When interacting with a person with greater dexterity, I'd watch closely for Ranger's signals that he wanted ear scritches or chin rubs and encourage the person to pet him there. A significant part of our job as handlers/partners is to interpret for our canine partner.

Partners/Handlers at Work

You and your dog are a team and the job is challenging for you as well. In addition to keeping track of all the factors that go into a visit and interpreting for their dogs, handlers/partners need to closely monitor their dogs. You'll be watching to make sure your dog is physically and mentally comfortable.

On a first visit it's very helpful to go with an experienced team. If that's not an option you may choose to accompany another dog/handler team without your canine partner before you and your dog start visiting as a team. If there are no available teams to shadow, you might want to visit the facility alone and do a brief walk through with the Life Enrichment Coordinator to make sure you're both on the same page and learn how the facility expects the visit to work.

As the human half of the team, there is a great deal for you to keep track of. You'll be remembering the specific visiting rules of the organization you belong to, learning the rules and expectations of the place you are visiting, and trying to make the human connection with the people you're visiting. You may be seeing distressing sights such as the bloody bandage around a recent amputation or smelling unpleasant smells of incontinence and recently cleaned up vomit. It can be intense. You'll also be watching your dog to keep them safe from such hazards as dropped pills or food that your dog might decide is a tasty snack. You'll be checking to see if your dog needs a drink or a break or to leave. You'll be juggling a lot of demands, details, and situations.

The first visit Ranger and I made was to a nursing home. We were guided around by someone from the Life Enrichment staff who seemed to take us to visit all the most heartbreaking residents. The one that stands out in memory is the resident sitting head thrown back, eyes vacant, and mouth gaping open in a silent scream. The Life Enrichment person assured us that the resident really loved dogs. I remember thinking to myself: "How can you tell; there's no one home." But I asked Ranger to sit next to the chair and the Life Enrichment staff picked up the resident's hand and placed it on Ranger's back. Over the course of a couple minutes something amazing happened. The silent scream shifted to a smile, presence came back into the eyes, and the hand began to stroke Ranger's fur. Wherever the resident had been wandering in a desolate internal landscape, the connection with Ranger was enough to fetch the person back into our space. It's a moment I will never forget; it was like watching a miracle in real time.

Ranger and I both left that visit exhausted. It was so challenging that I wondered if he would ever want to go back. We went to our next visit with me fully prepared for him to refuse to go in. The incredible moment with the one resident was enough to get me hooked, but I couldn't be sure Ranger felt the same way. I shouldn't have worried though. The next time we went he was pulling eagerly to go in and visit again.

There will, however, come a day when your previously eager-to-work dog will no longer want to work and will refuse to go. Or there may be a day you notice your dog doesn't seem to enjoy the work anymore or when you realize that your dog's health is becoming more fragile and they aren't physically up to the job anymore. That's the point when you'll realize that retirement is the best choice. You'll need to notify your Therapy Dog organization and the facilities you visit to let them know that your dog is retiring. Some facilities may want to hold a retirement party for your dog and ask you to make one more visit. You'll need to decide whether that is in the best interest of your dog. Some dogs may be ready for a final farewell visit but others may simply be finished working and that's all there is to it. Know your dog. Listen to your dog. Do what's best for your dog.

The saddest, and for me the hardest, part of having a Therapy Dog is the notifications you need to make when your dog dies. Therapy Dogs belong to you, but in a sense they belong to all the people they visit as well. The outpouring of grief that their passing engenders may be hard to bear on top of your own grief. When your Therapy Dog retires or when your Therapy Dog dies—and it is not uncommon for a Therapy Dog to work right up to near their end—you'll need to inform the organization with which they are associated and all the facilities where they visited.

Sometimes you'll already have a new Therapy Dog in training or already working in rotation with the retiring dog. You'll be able to continue visiting with the other dog. At my house we did have a second dog when Ranger crossed the Rainbow Bridge but she was absolutely not qualified or suitable to be a Therapy Dog. After nine months of grieving for Ranger we were ready to start looking around for his successor. Then one day, abruptly, our other dog was gone as well and we were dogless. A few months later I learned about a Great Pyrenees that needed to be rehomed due to changed family circumstances. I'd grown up with a pair of Great Pyrenees and love the breed, so I agreed we could meet the dog and see how it went. Shortly thereafter D'Artagnan joined our family and started his training to become a Therapy Dog.

Stress in Therapy Dogs Work

From time to time people who have a little bit of knowledge about canine body language will point to a Therapy Dog's lip licks, yawns, shake-offs, and stretches as indications that the dog is very stressed. The job is definitely stressful but it is important to remember that not all stress is bad. When you're working on a complex task and enjoying the challenge of getting it right, you experience a type of stress called eustress. Your awareness is heightened, your body is ready for action, and your mind is alert and focused. It feels good.

For the dog it is challenging but satisfying work and you will see stress signals from the dog as they manage the intensity of the job. While writing this book I've been experiencing plenty of eustress. It's been challenging, exciting, and just a little bit scary. It's a process I'm enjoying. If I keep at it for too long at a stretch however, the doubt badgers come to tear at me. I start to fear that I'll miss something important and to worry that I don't really know as much as I do. When the clawing of the doubt badgers becomes greater than the excitement and enjoyable challenge, I begin to experience distress. When that happens I know it's time to take a break. The same is true for our dogs. When they begin a visit they'll be excited, challenged, and maybe a little nervous; they're experiencing eustress.

I'm a big fan of giving my dogs choice to the greatest extent possible. At any point during a visit my dog can ask to quit and I'll honor that request. But even with the lip licks, yawns, shake-offs, etc., they don't ask to leave; they ask to visit one more person, to go into the next room to see the people there, to keep working. As their handler/partner we need to be careful to watch for signs that eustress is tipping over into distress. We never want our dogs to feel distress. Even though they may be asking to visit one more person, if we see distress developing we need to end the visit. If we insist that they keep working when that eustress begins slipping over into distress, we're not being the partner our dog needs.

It's up to us humans to know when to call it a day. We need to recognize when our dog has had enough. And we need to listen to our dogs when they show us signs they are becoming distressed. We are our dog's best advocate. Even when there are people wanting a visit or facility staff asking for just one more person to be seen, we need to heed our dog's signals. When our dog is done they are done.

Typically an experienced Therapy Dog can visit for about an hour. Dogs that are new to the job often need to stop after 15 or 20 minutes. When visiting with Ranger I'd usually start working our way toward the exit when we got close to the hour mark and by a few minutes after the hour we'd be out the door. We'd spend a few minutes talking and debriefing about the visit with the other teams outside the facility before heading home. Many days after leaving the facility and visiting outside, Ranger would suggest we could go back inside and visit more. I tried it once. I knew I was taking a tired dog back to work but I felt he was telling me he wanted to work more. I was curious if he really could, so I agreed. He lasted only about 10 more minutes before I started to see some stress panting; we learned that our typical visit length of a bit more than 60 minutes was best.

If you learn nothing else in this book, let it be this: You are the world's foremost expert on your dog, and it is your job to be the advocate for your dog. The most important thing you as a handler/partner do is to advocate for your dog. Your dog doesn't have words to say "I'm not feeling my best today and I'd like to go home now" or "I'm way too hot and I need a drink of water" or "This person is holding me too tightly and I don't like it." Your job is to listen to your dog and make sure they are getting the things that they need. It's not uncommon to want to visit one more person or to have the facilities person ask you to visit a little longer. It can be really hard to say no to just one more visit. We all want to visit just one more person, but we humans need to realize when our dog finished for the day and accept that. More than anything else, your job is to do right by your dog. And expecting a dog that isn't feeling great to visit people is just setting everyone up for failure and disappointment. Never ever push your dog to the point where they feel like they must say no with their teeth.

In addition to monitoring your dog for distress, you need to monitor and manage your own stress reactions. One of the reasons I like visiting as part of a group is the ability to alert the next team behind you. When the handler/partner in the next team knows what to expect, they can prepare themselves for a sight or smell that may be distressing or choose to bypass that room. Just like your dog you may find you are sliding from eustress to distress in the course of a visit. If that happens, you need to recognize it's time for you to call it a day.

What's Stressful About Visiting?

It seems strange that something that you and your dog are enjoying could turn into something distressing. Let's take a look at how that happens. The main culprit is something called trigger stacking. Remember the old saying about 'the straw that broke the camel's back'? More and more things were piled on the camel's back increasing the weight until that final straw was enough to break it. That's what trigger stacking is: all the little difficulties add together until it becomes too much. You experience the same thing yourself. Imagine you're running a little late. Add to that bad traffic and a near miss accident. Then when you get where you're going you realize you've parked in a puddle and the water sloshed into your shoe when you got out. You can shake off many of these things, but all together they're a challenge. If one more difficulty gets added, you may feel the need to scream.

Therapy dogs have a broad base of resilience to support the challenges of a visit but all the various things a dog is experiencing on a visit add up. The dog is probably overly warm, the floors are slippery, the facility is noisy, and it smells weird. The dog is most likely coping just fine with all of that, but if you add in something unexpected, it could be more than your dog can handle. It's these unexpected things that can cause our dogs to slide toward distress. These unexpected things might include unanticipated encounters with someone's reactive pet dog, or a visiting pet cat hiding behind a door, or, as happened to us on one visit, an animatronic cat in a room.

The animatronic cat was extremely lifelike in appearance and the sounds it made were very realistic, but it didn't quite move like a real cat and it definitely smelled wrong. The uncanny valley effect is well known in humans.[16] If you've ever seen something that was almost but not quite human, perhaps a Computer Generated Image (CGI) you may have been both fascinated and repelled. You were experiencing the uncanny valley. Dogs apparently react to that feeling that something is too close to being real while missing the mark as well. After the first dog was very unsettled by the not-quite-real cat, we decided to see how the other dogs felt. The amount of discomfort the dogs exhibited varied with some dogs being more puzzled and curious and some dogs objecting with barks and pulling away from it but none of them was unaffected. We learned it was best for our dogs to avoid the animatronic pets that are popular in Memory Care facilities. Although,

---

[16]

https://spectrum.ieee.org/automaton/robotics/humanoids/what-is-the-uncanny-valley

interestingly, the one time Ranger met an animatronic puppy it bothered him less than the animatronic cat.

Even if nothing unexpected happens and it's just the usual challenges of a visit, everything can add up over the length of the visit until that base of resilience is full leaving no room for anything else. This is true for humans and canines alike. You can monitor yourself and take the necessary steps to restore your resilience. But your dog is dependent on you to watch them and to listen to them so that you can prevent a slide into distress.

Chapter Four:
Necessary Qualities

To help you decide if you want to pursue Therapy Dog work, you'll need to determine whether you and your dog have the necessary temperament and resilience. Therapy Dog work isn't always easy and as we saw in the last chapter it really is work. In this chapter we'll examine the qualities needed by those that want to become Therapy Dog teams.

We'll start by looking at what the dog needs. Earlier I said it was clear soon after we adopted him that Ranger was born to be a Therapy Dog. I knew he was something special by how much Ranger loved people, all people. His greatest joy in life was meeting people. He wanted to interact with everyone he met. He was also possessed of a great charisma; everyone he met was instantly attracted to him. Even people who didn't care for dogs or were afraid of them responded to Ranger. He made friends everywhere he went.

The incident that really highlighted to me that he was born to be a Therapy Dog happened one day on a trip to the dog park. Ranger was a young, social, friendly, and playful dog. As a herding mix Ranger had endless energy and letting him play with his pals at the dog park was one way to burn off some of that energy. He loved going and was very adept at managing his canine social interactions. This particular day when I'd cued his release from the back of the car, he suddenly tore the leash out of my hand as I turned to close the car door and bolted down the hill to the park. When I caught up with him, he was in the car on the lap (all 90 pounds of him) of a woman we knew casually from the park. As I grabbed his leash intending to haul him off her I realized she was hugging him tightly and crying. She had just received some very bad news and while her own pair of dogs sat quietly in the backseat, Ranger was there providing comfort and support. I don't know if he could tell from the parking lot that she needed him or if he just ran off to visit a friend and discovered her on the way, but I do know he made a big difference for her when she needed it.

Qualities

So what were the qualities that made Ranger such an exceptional Therapy Dog? What were the qualities I was looking for in his successor? Summarizing the qualities is harder than I thought it would be. It's like the old line: I know it when I see it. But I'll do my best to identify the qualities that I believe are necessary to make a good Therapy Dog.

A Therapy Dog is calm and collected. They don't bounce around like jumping beans or race through the halls. The dog needs to be thoughtful and friendly. You want a dog that's genuinely fond of everyone and is figuring out how to connect with everyone they meet. You want a dog that wants to be touched, one that can never have enough petting. They're engaging and smart. A Therapy Dog needs to be confident and not easily overwhelmed.

A dog that indiscriminately adores everyone they meet can be a successful Therapy Dog but the smart dogs that are able to encourage people to engage with them have an extra edge. I've observed countless Therapy Dog evaluations. In one exercise the dogs are required to walk into a crowd of people, all of whom want to pet them. I've noticed that some dogs enter the crowd and are happy to let anyone pet them and some dogs enter the crowd and make sure everyone pets them. The smart dogs are the latter; they count how many people are in the crowd and how many of them have petted them. I love to see that. I may be a bit biased on the smart qualification, though. In my life I've lived with smart dogs and with those that aren't too bright. I far prefer the smart ones.

Ranger simply came with all the qualities needed to be the ideal Therapy Dog, and I didn't have to figure out what he needed to be. Let's take it from the other side, and examine what I was looking for in Ranger's successor. The first thing I was looking for was size. It's easier for dogs that are large or small to visit people in beds or wheelchairs. Medium-sized dogs are too big to lift easily and too small to be easily reached by people in wheelchairs or beds. This isn't to say they can't be Therapy Dogs, but medium-sized dogs take a bit more effort. Personally I have a great fondness for the giant dogs so I was looking for a very big dog.

The second thing I was looking for was temperament; I wanted a dog that was calm and easy-going, a dog that could take a lot of chaos in stride. The places dogs visit can be very busy with many different things going on. A dog that gets overwhelmed by that isn't going to enjoy Therapy Dog work. A dog that finds a busy facility interesting rather than nerve-wracking is going to be a much more relaxed and confident Therapy Dog.

The dog also needed to genuinely like people and love to be petted. This one should be pretty obvious. If the dog merely tolerates people and dislikes being touched, a job where lots of different people are touching them is really not going to be a good fit. But a dog that wants to say hello to everyone they meet and firmly believes you should pet them until your arm falls off is well suited for training for this job.

If your dog already has these qualities, you're in good shape. The two of you can get to work learning the skills you need to be an effective Therapy Dog Team. If your dog doesn't have these qualities or you don't currently have a dog, you'll need to find the right dog for Therapy Dog work. For some suggestions on how to find the right dog read on.

Puppies

Personally I prefer to start with an adult dog, but many people prefer to start with a puppy. If you decide you'd like to raise a puppy to be a Therapy Dog, you can maximize your chances of success by choosing a breed that is typically bred for friendliness and loving temperament. A Golden Retriever is a good example of this. You find a lot of Goldens doing Therapy Dog work. The next step is to carefullyselect the breeder and meet the parents of your puppy. Excellent breeders carefully consider temperament when selecting breeding pairs, and the temperament and behavior of the parents can help predict the eventual temperament and behavior of the puppy. When choosing the specific puppy, consult with the breeder about which puppy is most likely to excel at Therapy Dog work.

Once you have your puppy you will need to carefully socialize them. You want your puppy to learn that new experiences are interesting and fun rather than the puppy being afraid of new things. You socialize your puppy to enjoy new experiences by providing the emotional support they need as they learn how to approach new experiences. Socializing a puppy is more than simply taking them everywhere and exposing them to everything and expecting the puppy to figure it out and cope on their own. If you do that the puppy is unlikely to develop the resilience needed for Therapy Dog work. There are many excellent books on how to socialize a puppy in a positive and supportive fashion. I urge you to seek out these resources.

Your dog needs to be able to take new and novel experiences in stride because you never know what might happen on a Therapy Dog visit. On one group visit with Ranger, a resident fell in the hallway while we were visiting with people in a common room. We heard a loud crash as the resident and their wheelchair hit the floor followed by pained screams and the sound of running feet as staff converged to help. I was very pleased to see that all the dogs on that visit handled this frightening and unexpected event the same way. Each one of them initially oriented to the noise then checked with their partner/handler. Once the handler reassured them that the problem was being taken care of, the dogs went back to interacting with the person they'd been visiting. Even though the noise and chaos were right outside the door of the space they were in, they remained calm, relaxed, and focused on the job. That's the kind of behavior we want to see in a Therapy Dog and that sort of resilience is what you want to instill in your puppy.

While there are Therapy Dog organizations that will evaluate puppies, I am more comfortable with organizations that won't test a dog until they are at least a year old. Dogs go through a fear phase around eight months of age. Organizations that allow puppies to serve as Therapy Dogs are potentially putting dogs into environments they are not yet equipped to cope with. The dog is not being supported as they should be as they work through their teenage fear period; instead they are being expected to cope with all the chaos and unpredictability of a visit when they are most easily overwhelmed. In my opinion it simply isn't fair to the dog. I prefer organizations that will not test a dog until they have passed their first birthday. This gives a dog the best chance. While I've known several dogs that were ready for Therapy Dog work when they were a year old, it is more common for the dog to be older when they begin Therapy Dog work. Ranger was four when he passed his test.

The upside of starting with a puppy is that you will have control over all of his training and experience. You'll know every effort was made to give the puppy the skills and resilience they need to be a Therapy Dog. Puppies, however, are all potential and no certainty. Sometimes despite your best efforts, your carefully raised puppy just isn't suited to work as a Therapy Dog.

Adults

When you select an adult dog to train for Therapy Dog work you are able to see what you'll get in a way that isn't possible with a puppy. I wrote above about the qualities I looked for in choosing Ranger's successor. I wanted a calm, friendly, resilient dog able to take all sorts of things in stride.

Adult dogs can come from a variety of sources. They can be from shelters, breeders, fosters, owners, and rescues. Ranger came from an animal shelter but when I was looking for his successor, I was looking at rescues, specifically rescues that placed their dogs in foster homes. By choosing to adopt a dog from a foster home, I hoped to increase my chances of finding a dog that genuinely loved people. Animal shelters do amazing work but they don't always have a clear picture of a dog's personality since they are viewing the dog in the stressful shelter environment. A foster family that is living with the dog 24/7 should have a much better sense of the dog's personality in a home and community environment.

Of course dogs suitable for Therapy Dog work can come from anywhere. I've known lovely Therapy Dogs who started life as breeding bitches in puppy mills. I've also known wonderful Therapy Dogs who were retired champion show dogs. D'Artagnan came to us as a four-year-old rehome. The circumstances of his previous family had changed and although they loved him, they were no longer able to provide him with the care and attention he needed. Having been adopted as a puppy into a family with toddlers D'Artagnan came to us with great tolerance for chaos and unpredictability and with impeccable house manners. He already had some important skills. What he didn't have was a lot of experience in unfamiliar environments, and his obedience skills needed improvement.

Humans

Handlers/partners need certain skills and a special temperament as well. To do Therapy Dog work you need to genuinely enjoy other people. You need to have empathy that allows you to sense what others need but not the kind of empathy that has you carrying around another's unhappiness. You'll need to be friendly, calm, and approachable. These traits will make it easy for you to engage with the people you visit and easier for your dog to maintain their focus and enjoyment. Having a great relationship with your dog will be essential. As you engage in Therapy Dog work, you and your dog will be most effective if you are partners that can rely on each other. Let me give you an example of what that can look like.

I have an extremely poor sense of direction. But when we'd accompany new teams on their first visit, the handler/partners often complimented me on how well I knew my way around the facility. I have to confess that I really had no clue where we were, but I knew I could rely on Ranger. He knew exactly where to go and where everything was in each facility we visited. Ranger would act as my guide and I would act as his voice. He'd navigate us safely through the facility, and I'd make sure he got the kind of attention he wanted. We were partners with each of us doing what we were best suited to so we could be the most effective team possible.

To do Therapy Dog work you need to be responsible, reliable, and committed. If you've scheduled a visit, you need to be there unless you or your dog is sick. People are looking forward to your visit. For many of them seeing the Therapy Dogs may be the highlight of their month and if you don't show up, many people will be disappointed. In addition your failure to show up will reflect badly on you, your organization, and all the other teams that might want to visit there. It's important that you be able to multitask as well. You'll be supervising your dog, interacting with people, remembering facility rules, and minding the rules of your organization.

Therapy Dog work can be hard because you are visiting people that may not be there the next time you visit. Therapy Dog work often involves the aged, infirm, and medically fragile. You may also make hospice visits where you know the person you're visiting is nearing the end. You and your dog will become attached to certain people that you visit and when they are gone you will feel their loss deeply. This will be true of your dog as well; their favorite person to visit may not be there the next time. It can be hard. Sometimes, the dog has enjoyed Therapy Dog work but the handler/partner has found it too stressful. One handler/partner retiring from Therapy Dog work confessed to me that being so close in age to many of the people in the nursing home and visiting them felt too much like seeing their own future staring them in the face.

Doing Therapy Dog work may expose you to a lot of unpleasant sights, smells, and sounds that you'll need to take in stride. In addition you'll need to be okay with never knowing details or outcomes. For example, someone you are visiting may confide in you that they're scheduled for a risky surgery. You will not be able to call and find out how it went. HIPAA (Health Insurance Portability and Accountability Act) prevents facilities from giving out health information about their residents except to those the resident or guardian has specifically designated.

On one outdoor visit with my Therapy Dog group we witnessed a resident fall and strike their head on the concrete. We were not near the resident but it happened in clear sight of where we were. There was a lot of blood from the head wound and an ambulance was called. It was very upsetting to witness. The Activities Director had been unexpectedly called away before our visit. Someone else took over and accompanied us on our visit. The next day when the Activities Director called to check on how the visit had worked out, I asked if she could tell us how the resident that had fallen was doing. After thinking it over, the Activities Director decided that since we knew nothing about the resident, not even a name, it was within the bounds of HIPAA to tell us the resident was home from the hospital. This was an exception; usually you'll have no idea how something turned out.

It may seem like this chapter spent a lot of time dwelling on the less enjoyable aspects of Therapy Dog work. I am not trying to put you off Therapy Dog work, but simply to present the downside realities and the qualities that will enable you and your dog to accept these realities and enjoy the positive difference you'll make as a Therapy Dog team. It is hard work but it is incredibly satisfying. You'll be improving the physical, mental, and emotional health of those you visit, which is a pretty great result.

Chapter Five:
Important Skills

When I'm asked what skills a successful Therapy Dog needs, I always answer the same way. In my opinion the most fundamental skill a Therapy Dog needs is impeccable manners. By "manners" I mean being able to conduct themselves in a calm and polite fashion when interacting in the human world. The American Kennel Club (AKC) in their Canine Good Citizen (CGC)[17] test has done a good job of capturing what these good manners look like. Most, if not all, Therapy Dog tests incorporate aspects of the CGC. In fact, Therapy Dogs International has built its entire test[18] around the CGC adding elements that are specific to Therapy Dog work such as reactions to such medical equipment as wheelchairs, walkers, etc.

---

[17] American Kennel Club. "An Owner's Manual for: by the AMERICAN KENNEL CLUB 10 ESSENTIAL SKILLS: CGC TEST ITEMS."

[18] Therapy Dogs International. *Therapy Dogs International (TDI) Testing Requirements.* tdi-dog.org.

Basic Good Manners

Good manners include such things as walking on a loose leash. A dog that's walking next to you on a loose leash is unlikely to pull you off balance, catch the leash on a piece of equipment and pull it over, or be so focused on getting where they're going that they aren't paying attention to anything else. Walking on a loose leash is also a valuable skill when someone you're visiting wants to walk your dog. Ranger and I regularly visited an adult daycare program where one of the participants loved nothing more than to hold Ranger's leash and walk around. With my dogs I use what is called a traffic grip leash, which is a six-foot leash with an extra handle loop right next to the collar clip. I could hook a finger into that loop and allow the participant to hold the handle at the end and we'd walk all around the space. The participant was so proud to be able to 'walk' the big dog, but I still had connection and control the entire time.

A polite well mannered dog will respond promptly and willingly to basic cues like sit, down, and stay. When you're visiting a facility, your dog needs to follow cues to sit in a position that is easy for someone to reach and to stay there. With a big dog, for example, it's helpful if they sit beside a person rather than in front. When they sit beside the chair they're less likely to step on the person's feet. With experience a dog will be able to figure out for themselves which position is most convenient for the person they are visiting, but in the beginning you'll need to help them out. 'Sit,' 'down,' and 'stay' can also double as tricks. People are delighted to see dogs perform even these basic behaviors on cue.

It's best that, on a visit, you never leave your Therapy Dog in someone else's charge, but sometimes you are left with no other choice. Sometimes you may need to run back to your car for something you forgot and you don't have the time to put on and take off your dog's raincoat again. (Yes, it's a good idea for your dog to have a raincoat so they don't arrive soaking wet for a visit. No one enjoys touching a wet dog.) Or perhaps you need to use a very tiny restroom where there isn't room for both you and your dog. Because I love big dogs, this has happened to me. It's also possible that the facility doesn't want dogs in the restroom. If something like this happens, your dog will need to stay calmly and willingly with another person while you are out of sight.

People unfamiliar to the dog should be able to pet them in a variety of ways without the dog becoming stressed. This should hold true whether it is one person or a group of people. As a Therapy Dog your dog will frequently be surrounded by several people all trying to pet them at once. As a result the dog should be comfortable in a crowd of people all reaching toward them at the same time. Your dog may find themselves hemmed in by wheelchairs and walkers on every side. Or, as happened when Ranger and I were visiting a college campus during a finals week stress reduction visit, the dog may be swarmed with people petting every part of him they can reach. A dog that doesn't get overwhelmed by that level of attention is going to be much more suitable for doing Therapy Dog work than one that is nervously trying to keep track of everyone around them.

Some Therapy Dog teams work alone, while others visit as part of a group of Therapy Dogs visiting at the same time. Whether you're alone or part of a group, your dog should have no problem meeting another friendly dog. They should also be able to ignore another dog that is working there. Pet visitation policies vary widely between facilities. You never know for sure what you may encounter in the hallways. One facility Ranger and I went to often had a Great Pyrenees visiting who was reactive to other dogs. When we knew the Pyrenees was also visiting we'd work at avoiding him. I knew, however, that if we did accidentally meet, Ranger would stay calm and not react even if he got barked at. Having a dog that is calm in the presence of other dogs makes a visit more relaxed and pleasant.

On a visit you may need to consult with a staff member or you may bump into someone you know and want to talk to them for a bit. You should be able to freely meet and interact with others without your dog becoming a pest or getting distressed. A dog that keeps trying to solicit attention or drag you away to go visit someone is an annoying pest. Dogs that act like that remind me of badly behaved toddlers.

Therapy Dogs experience a lot of different situations. If they listen to kids read at a school, they may get caught in the hallway as classes are let out for recess and be subjected to a mass of kids in a hurry to get outside. They might be present during a medical emergency where people are rushing to help. To be a successful Therapy Dog your dog will need to remain calm and under control in the presence of children or adults running and yelling. Or, as happened to Ranger and me, they may be visiting at the same time the facility is testing the fire alarm. Sudden loud noises and unpredictable fast movement are things a Therapy Dog needs to be prepared to handle. Basically, when training a Therapy Dog, you want your dog to be calm and well mannered in any situation.

Good Manners for Therapy Dogs

The items above are basic good manners that should serve any dog that goes out in public. It's time now to turn our attention to some of the specific good manners a Therapy Dog needs when visiting a healthcare facility. The first of these is that your dog needs to be comfortable around a wide range of medical equipment. Some dogs can be unnerved by people on wheels or people using walkers that look like extra clomping legs in front or people leaning on that perfectly good stick that would be better used for fetch. During their initial training whenever we'd see someone using a wheelchair, walker, or cane, I'd encourage my dogs to watch from a safe distance. And when my dogs told me they were ready to meet the person, I'd ask if they'd like to meet my dog. This is how I got my dogs used to seeing the most common pieces of medical equipment they'd be exposed to on visits. Once we started visiting I used the same technique of letting the dog examine from a safe distance when we'd see equipment they were unfamiliar with. Medicine and food carts rumbling down hallways can be unsettling, and giant floor buffers can seem like monsters shrieking along. But because we'd worked hard on laying a good foundation, we've been able to safely and successfully navigate those hazards.

A word of warning here about keeping your dog safe around wheeled things. Many dogs will sit with their tail stretched out behind them. As Ranger and I learned the hard way, this can be dangerous to the dog. People pushing carts or using wheelchairs may not see the dog's tail. Fortunately for us Ranger and I learned this by simply having hair on the end of his tail yanked out and not by having the last few bones in his tail crushed. Keep your dog's tail safe. When your dog is sitting, gently nudge their tail into a position where it's wrapped around their feet and not stretched out behind them.

Another important skill you'll need your dog to have is a rock solid 'leave it' cue. When you are able to tell your dog to ignore something either verbally or with a hand signal and have your dog heed it, you have another tool for keeping your dog safe. It's common to see spilled food or even the occasional lost pill on the floor when you're visiting. If you see a pill, be sure to report that to staff. A rock solid 'leave it' cue means you can be certain that your dog won't consume the dropped food or lost pill. This can be either because you've cued them to leave it or because you've trained them to never pick anything up off the floor. This can actually save your dog's life. It seems like at least once a year I hear about a Therapy Dog that has died from ingesting a pill they found on a visit. The 'leave it' cue is also useful when your visit coincides with the end of meal time and plates and trays are being collected and stashed in carts to return to the kitchen. Dirty plates and leftovers in a cart are conveniently at nose height for all sizes of dogs. A solid 'leave it' is a really useful cue when your dog realizes just how convenient.

Additional Helpful Training

One of the things I've found very helpful for my dogs to know is a 'paws up' cue. Sometimes a dog will need to place their front paws on a chair or the edge of a bed to make themselves tall enough for the person to reach. Often you'll find residents in a bed that has been jacked up very high. For small dogs a bed visit is possible but for a large dog it works best to have them put their paws on something to make themselves tall enough to reach. Putting a chair next to the bed and asking the dog to 'paws up' on the seat of the chair usually works to make a large dog tall enough for even someone in a very high bed to reach and touch.

It's also helpful for Therapy Dogs to know some tricks. These can be classic tricks such as shaking hands or spinning but even 'sit' and 'down' can entertain an audience. Ranger had two cues that never failed to get a positive reaction. He could 'speak' and 'bark.' For the 'speak' cue he would open and close his mouth as if barking and sometimes make a tiny noise. "Bark" was his cue to let out one loud woof. After asking him to speak I would praise him with "That's right; inside we speak quietly" and after a bark I'd tell him that barking belonged outside. Ranger enjoyed the laughter we got for this routine. People love to see dogs perform tricks. They needn't be elaborate or complex tricks; even very simple tricks that you may not even think of as a trick can delight people.

My current Therapy Dog, D'Artagnan, is a Great Pyrenees, a notoriously independent minded breed. He received his credentials literally the day before all Therapy Dog visits were suspended due to a global pandemic. When our state loosened some restrictions, facilities asked us to do dog parade visits. In these visits the residents would gather socially distanced from one another outside in many areas around the building. One dog at a time would go to a space visible to the gathered residents and perform while the Life Enrichment Coordinator read some biographical notes about that dog and introduced their tricks. Knowing D'Artagnan's tendency to get bored with repetition and thus refuse to do his tricks of 'sit,' 'down,' and 'bounce' repeatedly, I included in his biography the joke "Why should you never give a Great Pyrenees a cue more than once? Because he ignored you just fine the first time." Then when he performed his tricks, the audience was delighted to see him do what he was asked. If he didn't perform, they were entertained that they'd just seen the joke happen in real life. I'm convinced dogs can tell when an audience is responding to them and I'm certain that by the end D'Artagnan was reading the audience to see whether complying with the cue or ignoring it would play better.

Another thing that people seem to really enjoy is dogs dressed in costumes. Before you dress your dog in a costume, please make sure your dog enjoys dressing up. And please be careful to make sure that your dog can move freely in whatever costume you put on them. The other thing to monitor is your dog's temperature; you need to make sure your dog isn't getting overheated. Facilities for fragile and aged populations tend to be kept at warmer temperatures than most people are accustomed to. I learned pretty early on to dress lightly for visits to nursing homes, especially in winter. Even if not wearing a costume, a dog can get very warm on visits. I carry a collapsible water bowl with me so I can give my dog a drink if he needs it.

A lot of delightful costumes are available for small dogs, but with a little creativity it's possible to dress up even a giant dog. For my giant dogs I've found that novelty headbands for people make a quick and easy costume. My dog can show up with antlers, monster eyes, or whatever is seasonally appropriate. At Halloween I've put a headband with monster eyes over his collar and another headband facing the opposite direction just before his hips. This became a super simple monster costume that was comfortable for him to wear, amusing for residents, and did not make him warmer.

I hope this chapter has given you a sense of the kind of things a Therapy Dog needs to learn and why those skills are important. In all honesty all the skills and behaviors described are useful even for a simple pet. However, all of these skills and behaviors go into developing an exceptional Therapy Dog.

Chapter Six: Set Your Dog Up for Success

In the last chapter we talked about the skills that a Therapy Dog needs. While I won't be offering detailed instructions on how to teach the cues and behaviors identified in Chapter Five, I do want to share some of the foundational training I use to help my dogs prepare for Therapy Dog work. Just like any other job or structured activity Therapy Dogs need training. They need to acquire and practice the skills and behaviors that will help them excel as Therapy Dogs. In this chapter we'll focus on the foundation training that a Therapy Dog needs.

Train So the Dog Can Succeed

For me the bottom line in training is that I want my dogs to have the skills to be successful when navigating the human world. The more I can communicate to them the rules of specific situations, the more they are equipped to handle the situation. I want my dogs to feel like they have control over what they do and how they interact with their world. The feeling of being in control is powerfully reinforcing for all species. In her book *The Science of Consequences: How They Affect Genes, Change the Brain, and Impact the World* author Susan M. Schneider describes a study in which deer mice, a species that didn't like the light, were taught to turn on and turn off a light switch. The sense of control this gave the rodents was so powerful, they would run to one side of the space to turn on the light in order to run to the other side and turn it back off.[19] One way I give my dogs that feeling of control is through communication. My dogs are able to say no to things that they don't like.

Communicating with my dog is the bedrock of how and what I train. When a dog knows that they are free to say no, it makes it easier for the dog to say yes. It's true for people too. Imagine you're going somewhere necessary but not very enjoyable; for a lot of people this might be the doctor or dentist. Chances are that you take a minute before getting out of the car

---

[19] Schneider, Susan M., The Science of Consequences: How They Affect Genes, Change the Brain, And Impact the World, 2012, Prometheus Books, Amherst, New York, pp. 27-28.

to remind yourself why you need to go. Or maybe you stop and take a deep breath before you open the door to go in. At each step you've had the chance to change your mind and not go through with it; you're in control. Then when you begin interacting with the doctor or dentist, you're told what you need to do to cooperate which allows you to retain some control. For example, you don't open your mouth for the dentist until you're prepared to consent to the dental exam. I believe we should do our best to give our dogs that same sense of control and consent.

A dog that's asked to interact with someone who is connected to medical equipment that is beeping and flashing may need to pause before deciding if this is something they want to do. That equipment may seem worrisome to the dog and they may need to think about it for a minute. When the dog stops at the doorway to the room with all the equipment beeping and flashing, as handler/partners we have a choice. We can use the leash to drag the dog into the room or we can give the dog the minute they need to choose. And we can respect their choice even when it is saying no to the visit. When a dog knows they are free to take a minute and that a refusal will be respected, they're much more likely to choose to approach and enjoy interacting with something novel. I'm a big fan of consent training where the dog is free to choose to participate or not. It makes for a much happier and more emotionally balanced and secure dog when they know they have control of their choices.

Therapy Dogs need to freely engage with a wide variety of people. Many people train their dogs not to approach other people and solicit attention. Since this training is at odds with the job of a Therapy Dog, it is useful to train a 'visit' or 'say hello' cue. When your dog has a cue letting them know that the choice to visit and solicit attention is now in their control, your dog is empowered to do their job. Personally, I train my dogs with the goal of being a Therapy Dog so I allow them to greet anyone they wish and solicit attention from them as long as the person is willing and the dog is polite. Knowing my dogs will be Therapy Dogs, I train a 'no visit' cue telling the dog when they must stay with me and not greet or solicit other people.

Whether you have trained your dog to wait for your cue to visit or to choose on their own whether to visit, it's important that they wait for an invitation or a cue before approaching people. This invitation can be given by you or by the person requesting the visit. Invitations by others can take the form of smiling at the dog and trying to make eye contact with them. If your dog is trained to wait for your cue, you'll need to watch for these subtle indications that a person is asking for a visit and cue your dog accordingly. One of the reasons I like letting my dogs visit as they choose is because they are much better at picking up on these signs than I am. Either way, you are giving your dog the information they need to understand the context in which they are functioning. Giving your dog the information they need is an essential component of good training.

Socialization

Whether you're training a puppy or an adult dog, the emphasis will be on socialization, resilience, and coping with novelty. Your goal is to build confidence. One way I like to build confidence and resilience is to expose my dogs to lots of novel things. This doesn't mean simply dropping a dog into an unfamiliar experience, strange place, or confusing circumstance and hoping they can figure out how to cope. It means giving careful and thoughtful introduction to things outside the dog's normal routine.

I've learned that hardware stores, auto repair places, and of course pet supply stores are good places to work on socialization with your dog. It's polite to call first and make sure the store is dog friendly. If it is, your dog can meet new people and receive attention from them. The dog can experience walking next to a shopping cart. And they can experience meeting and ignoring unfamiliar dogs. When training Ranger I also discovered that if you ask nicely, often a doctor's office will allow you to bring your Therapy Dog in training into the waiting room while you pay your bill. With a little thought you can find many places to visit with your dog as you work on training them for Therapy Dog work.

Training Philosophy in Practice

It's probably helpful at this point to use my current Therapy Dog, D'Artagnan, as an example of what I mean. Before he came to live with me, he was a well loved pet of a young family. His life was full of familiar routines and well known places without a lot of novelty. When he first came to live with us everything was novel for him: new people, new house, new yard, new neighborhood, and feline housemates. Initially we introduced regular training sessions to work on his basic obedience and helped him to become familiar with his new world. As he became more habituated to life with us, we began slowly expanding it.

With his world and life with us now familiar and routine, we continued training the basic obedience skills needed to pass a Therapy Dog test and added new experiences. Some of these experiences were as simple as going for a walk somewhere he'd never been before. As a Livestock Guardian Dog, Great Pyrenees are bred to live with stock and protect them from predators. In this capacity a Great Pyrenees will move with the stock from pasture to pasture. They need to learn the terrain of each place. When we first began taking D'Artagnan on walks in unfamiliar places, we could see him beginning to build a map in his head. He would doze lightly in the back of the car while on roads we'd been on before and he would sit up to watch when we turned onto a road he hadn't been on before. D'Artagnan was starting to think and use his brain in ways it was designed to be used but that hadn't been a necessary part of his life until now.

As more places became familiar to him we began to add experiences that actually pushed him a bit out of his comfort zone. We would visit empty playgrounds and ask him to climb on the climbing platforms or walk on the short suspension bridges. We paid attention to the different surfaces that were available and made sure he knew how they felt under his paws. We walked on the beach with the water nearly lapping his paws. At any point he could refuse to try something that was too far out of his comfort zone and we would accept that, but most things we asked he was willing to try with a bit of coaxing. He was never forced to do something he considered beyond his ability to cope with, but with each new thing he successfully managed, his confidence grew a little bit.

One new experience we offered him was walking down a boat ramp. Boat ramps are steep and frequently made of open metallic mesh. Sometimes they're made of wood and can be quite slippery so have traction bars or sandpaper rough strips to provide people with better footing. The first time we invited him to walk on a boat ramp D'Artagnan flat out refused so we simply walked away and did something else. The next time we offered, he was willing to put one paw on it before refusing and again we simply took him walking somewhere else. We never forced him to do more than he was willing to do. Over the course of a summer he gained confidence until he was asking to walk down boat ramps and out onto floating docks. I like having a dog walk on a floating dock. I don't have any scientific evidence for it but I believe the feeling of the surface shifting and rocking prepares them for Therapy Dog visits that involve elevators. By walking on a floating dock a dog learns that surfaces can move and that this is something they can handle. I think it makes that first elevator ride a little less intimidating.

All along D'Artagnan was learning that he could do novel things. He was learning that we would support him and that he could trust us to listen to him if he refused. He was learning that we'd be patient and give him the time he needed to figure things out and that we wouldn't force or rush him. We'd had him nearly a year when we were taking a hike and he was confronted with a boardwalk missing several boards. He studied the situation for a time then confidently led the way across. When we'd first adopted him, he would not have felt confident on that boardwalk and we would have had to turn back. He'd developed a lot more confidence and resilience. He understood that he could manage unfamiliar things.

In his book *Eye of the Trainer* Ken Ramirez devotes one section to the intelligence he's seen demonstrated by highly trained animals.[20] I don't think that it's only training that brings out this intelligence. I believe that the more an animal is encouraged to think, the smarter and better problem solvers they become. So all the training I do with my dogs emphasizes them thinking and figuring out. They learn interesting things and get lots of opportunities to practice problem solving with enriching puzzles, searches, and novelty. The more we train our dogs and teach them that they can do novel things, the

---

[20] Ramirez, Ken, "The Eye of the Trainer: Animal Training, Transformation, and Trust," Karen Pryor Clicker Training Sunshine Books, Inc., Waltham, MA., 2020, p. 205-209.

more they know and the more they think. The more they think the more creative they can become.

Ranger demonstrated that principle at a local pet supply store. The store was holding a little fun fair and dogs were completing a trick course to win prizes. One of the tricks was to do a 'paws up' on an inverted plastic tub. Ranger looked at the tub and decided there was no way it would support his weight. I agreed that he was right to be cautious so asked him to demonstrate 'paws up' on a nearby chair then planned to go on to the next trick. Ranger had other ideas. After doing a beautiful 'paws up' on the chair, he refused to go on to the next trick but stood studying the plastic tub. Suddenly Ranger went into a 'down' and propped his front paws up on the tub. He'd solved the problem of the tub not being strong enough to support his weight while still managing to have his paws up on the tub.

Giving Dogs Control

Earlier I mentioned control and choices. If you think about it dogs aren't typically given much control or many choices. They're told what to eat, when to go out, where to be, where to walk, etc. Virtually every part of their life is under someone else's control. Where possible I like to give my dogs as much control and as many choices as I reasonably can. D'Artagnan can be inside or outside during the day. I do make him sleep inside at night, to his disgust. I let him out in the morning and when he wants to come in he knocks on the door. When he wants to go out again, he'll tell one of us. And that's the nice thing: he has learned that he can tell us what he wants. Since I don't always understand when my dogs tell me something, they become familiar with the question, "Can you show me what you want?" They get very good at doing that. Sometimes I expect that D'Artagnan will show me that he'd like to go out, but instead he'll stop at the place his chews are kept and put his nose on a particular package. It's clear he's saying, "I'd like one of these." When that happens I give him the chew he's asked for.

Every time we listen to our dogs, every time we support them when they try something new, every time they learn that they can do new and strange things, it builds their confidence and resilience a little more. This is how I create the attributes that go into a successful Therapy Dog and a canine companion that is a partner and friend.

Chapter Seven: Understanding Rules and Requirements

Thinking about how we care for our dogs, how we equip them, and what we feed them doesn't seem like something that needs an entire chapter. After all, everyone wants to care for their dog in the best way they can. But when you belong to a Therapy Dog organization, you'll discover they have rules that touch on how to care for your dog, what equipment can be used with your dog, and even what your dog should eat. Many of these rules will be the best practice for caring for your dog. Other rules are dictated by the Therapy Dog organization's insurance carrier. And some of the rules are controversial. The latter include rules that are applied to all teams due to particular health risks in a particular region and rules about what you may feed your dog. There's a lot to learn and to keep track of.

Good Practice Rules

Canine Good Health

Let's begin with the things that are simply good practice. Dogs need to be in excellent health. A reputable Therapy Dog organization will monitor the health of the dog. They'll require an annual vet health check and that the dog be current on all vaccines. Good organizations should also accept titer testing in lieu of vaccines except for those vaccines, such as rabies, that are mandated by law. Not only is it common sense to make sure your pet dog stays healthy and problems are caught before they become serious, but this is especially important for a Therapy Dog. Some zoonotic diseases can pass from animals to people and vice versa. Maintaining your dog in the best health protects both the dog and the people they visit.

Coercion Free

The next bit of good practice is to always choose force free training and practices. No reputable Therapy Dog organization will allow a dog to test or be worked on any sort of coercive equipment. Therapy

Dogs should never be under any sort of coercion. In order to do their work effectively they need to be happy to work, not forced to work. Reputable Therapy Dog organizations will prohibit the use of nose bands, choke chains, restrictive harnesses, and prong collars during visits. Such coercive tools have no place in Therapy Dog work.

A Therapy Dog should be worked on a flat buckle collar or non-restrictive harness and leash. Some organizations require the use of a four-foot leash and others of a leash no longer than six feet. The point of requiring a leash of fixed length rather than a retractable leash is that retractable leashes tend to provide confusing signals to the dog while a fixed length leash does not. Retractable leashes can also be very dangerous to people and other dogs if misused.

Most people think of a collar and leash first and foremost as a management tool, but I find it more effective to think of it as a communication tool. Using the leash for communication is most important in Therapy Dog work. Messages can travel up and down the leash keeping a team in constant touch. I like to use a traffic grip leash with my dogs. It's convenient because my Therapy Dogs are large. A traffic grip leash is a six-foot leash with another handle loop directly off the clip. I think of using this handle as the equivalent of holding a small child's hand. It tells my dog that I need them to stay very close. The standard I aspire to is to be able to replace the leash with a piece of string and have as much connection and control of my 103-pound dog as when I use the six-foot nylon leash. I'm not there yet with D'Artagnan but we're working on meeting that aspiration. I never actually tried it with Ranger but I believe we could have done it.

Therapy Dogs should always be on leash when working. Some organizations will make exceptions to this rule if a dog is performing for an audience on a visit. Therapy Dogs should work on a leash to maintain the connection between handler/partner and dog. The unexpected often happens on Therapy Dog visits. It might be someone latching onto the dog's collar and refusing to let go or it may be someone hugging the dog extra tightly and making them feel trapped. If you and your dog are used to relying on the leash to communicate, then during such an unexpected and unsettling experience your dog won't feel abandoned and alone. The dog will know you're still there and working to get them free.

When we began Therapy Dog work I heard a number of stories about people latching onto the Therapy Dog's collar and refusing to let go. As I pictured how unsetting it would be for Ranger to have a stranger latched onto his collar pulling it against his neck in unpredictable ways, I thought about ways to protect him from this. I decided to keep Ranger's collar loose enough that he could back out of it should it be necessary and I taught him a 'back' cue. In all the visits we did, there was only once I thought I was going to need this 'back' cue to get him to back out of his collar. The person he was visiting had latched onto his head and collar. I could see him getting more and more uncomfortable and was just opening my mouth to tell him 'back' when the person saw a different dog and released Ranger to reach for the other dog. I'm happy I never needed to use his 'back' cue but I'm glad I had it ready. An important part of being a handler/partner is to be prepared for unexpected things that might happen and have ways to manage them.

Dogs are very situational learners. We can take advantage of this and establish specific identifiers for what the dog will be doing. One way we're able to do this is by having a special collar and leash that is only used for Therapy Dog work. I pair my dog's harness and leash with their official organization bandanna. Talk to Therapy Dog people and you'll hear countless stories about dogs getting excited when they see their working gear of bandanna or vest. I like having a special collar and leash that I pair with the bandanna my dogs wear. They quickly learn that both pieces, collar with leash and bandanna, must be present or it doesn't mean going to work. That means I can wash and iron the bandanna without triggering excitement.

Easy to Recognize

It's important that a working Therapy Dog team be easily identifiable. Organizations will require some sort of identifying apparel for the dogs and handler/partners. Some Therapy Dog organizations have dogs wear identifying vests when visiting. I prefer the philosophy that Therapy Dogs are there to be petted and we should have as few barriers between the person and the dog as practical. To achieve this many organizations have their Therapy Dogs wear an identifying bandanna and/or a collar tag. The dogs are easily identifiable in their bandannas and tags while also having lots of available fur to pet.

For partner/handlers some organizations require a uniform shirt or vest while others require a simple name tag. One way or another dogs and handlers/partners should be clearly identifiable regardless of whether the dogs wear vests, bandannas, or tags and the people wear uniforms or name badges. Each organization wants its members to be clearly recognizable and for all its teams to be a credit to the organization.

When you're visiting you should represent your organization in a positive fashion. You and your dog should both be clean, well groomed, and well mannered. You want to make a good impression. You want the facility to invite you to come back. You want the facility to invite other dogs from your organization to visit. If you make a poor impression you won't be invited back and neither will anyone else from your organization. You are the representative of your organization.

Use of Treats

We all know dogs love food and that people love to feed dogs. When you're visiting you'll find people who keep dog treats on hand just to feed the dogs. However, most Therapy Dog organizations have rules about the use of treats on a visit and these rules don't allow everyone to give the dog treats. Dogs can get very excited in the presence of treats and can become so focused on the prospect of a treat that they ignore everything else. That's not behavior we want from Therapy Dogs. So training treats and treats from those the dog is visiting are usually prohibited. The most common exception is reinforcement treats if the dog has been performing. A dog doing a trick exhibition or similar performance may receive treats, in other words.

When we'd run into someone who insisted on Ranger having a treat, I would take the treat and ask Ranger to do a trick to earn it. This seemed to be a reasonable compromise. The person was able to see that Ranger got his treat and Ranger knew that he'd have to show off to earn a reward.

A Go Bag is Useful

A useful tip is to maintain a bag filled with things that you want to have with you when going on a Therapy Dog visit. I call it my go bag and in it I have a clean and pressed bandanna, the special collar and leash, extra poop bags, my identification, a full water bottle, a collapsible water bowl, grooming rake, hand sanitizer, handouts such as business cards for our Therapy Dog group, coloring pages, bookmarks, and/or business cards with my dog's photo on them to give to children that read to him, and some pet grooming wipes. I keep the blanket my dog lies on when listening to kids read with the bag. I like to wash the blanket between uses.

Most of the things in the go bag are pretty self-explanatory but I'd like to explain a couple of them. One of our regularly scheduled visits happened just before a Farmer's Market. I would often take Ranger with me when I'd drop by to do some shopping, I would leave Ranger in his working gear so that he would know he was still free to work and could provide a bit of extra publicity for our organization. As a result we'd get questions about Therapy Dog work so it was nice to have business cards to hand out. We made these cards so they could be used by anyone in the group. We included basic information and the Therapy Dog website link on one side and space for individual information on the reverse.

When kids were reading to Ranger they were always delighted to receive a little extra reward. Over the course of his working life Ranger had bookmarks, trading cards, and mini business cards with different photos of him on one side and a message about how much Ranger had liked listening to the reader on the other. D'Artagnan will have coloring pages as well as mini business cards and bookmarks. I might even design him his own trading card. Organizations typically don't supply these, but many handlers/partners choose to create and purchase them on their own. It's not a requirement but the kids enjoy them.

I include grooming wipes in my go bag for a couple of reasons. First, of course, is to maintain good hygiene. It's a good idea to wipe down your dog after a visit. This helps prevent the spread of germs and also helps to settle your dog after work. If you live in an area with snow and ice, your dog will end up walking through de-icing chemicals. Some of these chemicals are toxic so you don't want your dog to lick them off their paws. Some of the chemicals can burn your dog's paws. By wiping their paws clean when they enter a facility and when they are back in the car you're protecting the dog from injury.

Because I have a special affinity for dogs with longer coats, I keep a grooming rake in my go bag. I want my dogs to look good when they visit and longer coats pick up more debris than a smooth coat. Dogs should be clean and well groomed as should the handler/partners. The appearance of both of you should be a credit to the organizations you are representing. I prefer organizational rules that let you determine how often your dog needs to be bathed but some organizations stipulate that a dog should be bathed within 24 hours of a visit.

Insurance-Driven Rules

In order to provide liability insurance coverage for members, Therapy Dog organizations often adopt rules that aren't based on scientific evidence or well documented problems. Instead these rules are adopted at the behest of the insurance carrier. Adopting these insurance-driven rules can reduce the price of the liability policy covering all active volunteers. The two most common of these rules are a refusal to approve registered Service Dogs as Therapy Dogs and a refusal to evaluate or approve dogs that are Schutzhund trained or trained as Police or Military Working Dogs. Schutzhund trained dogs are dogs that are trained for tracking, obedience, and protection. This includes bite-work.

A registered Service Dog is likely already covered by a liability insurance policy that is held by the organization that has registered the Service Dog. If the dog is also a registered Therapy Dog and something happens on a visit that triggers an insurance payout, it would be complicated to determine which insurance policy was in effect at the time. The question will be whether the incident happened because the dog was acting in their capacity as a Service Dog or their capacity as a Therapy Dog. By refusing to register a dog that is a registered Service Dog, the potential issue is avoided.

The thing insurance companies appear to fear most is a Therapy Dog losing control and biting someone. Police and Military Working Dogs and dogs trained to compete in Schutzhund are all dogs that are trained to bite when directed to. Insurance companies fear that if a dog has been trained to bite, they will be more likely to bite. As a result Therapy Dog organizations are strongly discouraged from allowing these dogs to be evaluated as Therapy Dogs. This can be frustrating for people who would like to do Therapy Dog work with their retired Police or Military Working Dog or their Schutzhund competing dog.

All organizations require that you report to them any incident that may trigger an insurance claim. If your dog accidentally scratches someone and they bleed, it should be reported. If your dog knocks over a piece of equipment by accident, it should be reported. Anything that happens on a visit that could potentially trigger an insurance claim should be reported to your organization and to the facility if you are visiting without escort. If you are accompanied by a member of staff when an incident occurs, the staff member should make note of it for the facility and you should report it to your organization.

Controversial Rules

One Size Applies to All Rules

Therapy Dog organizations that register dogs nationally or internationally are caught in the unenviable position of making rules for all the dogs that are registered with their organization. It's easier to apply a rule to everyone in an organization than to define the parameters of where it applies. For example, in parts of the southwestern United States heartworm is a serious problem while in the Pacific Northwest the problem is generally rare. When situations like this occur a Therapy Dog organization that registers dogs in both places must address the problem happening in the Southwest. The organization will do this by adopting a rule stipulating that all dogs registered with the organization must be on a heartworm preventative and tested regularly. For the people in the Southwest this falls under the heading of good practice while for people in the Northwest it constitutes an additional financial burden and the need to medicate their dog when not strictly necessary. One size seldom fits all and Therapy Dog organizations are forced to do the best they can to meet the needs and expectations of their teams and the facilities these teams will visit.

Raw Feeding Rules

Quite a few Therapy Dog organizations have rules about what your dog is fed. This is probably the most controversial of the rules Therapy Dog organizations adopt. Several organizations will not accept dogs that are fed a raw diet. The American Veterinary Medical Association does a nice job of laying out why a Therapy Dog organization would have concerns about the potential health risks a raw fed dog might pose to young children and elderly people.

> One of the important concerns that drove the development of this policy is the concern that therapy animals fed raw diets and taken into hospitals, nursing homes or other healthcare facilities could serve as sources of infection to patients whose immune system may already be compromised by illness.[21]

---

[21] "Raw Pet Foods and the AVMA's Policy: FAQ." *American Veterinary Medical Association*, www.avma.org/raw-pet-foods-and-avmas-policy-faq.

These are valid concerns. However, people who feed a raw diet are adamant that feeding raw food is the healthiest diet for their dog. There is scientific evidence that shows that it is a healthy diet.[22] The problem, of course, is that the "raw food is best" research and the "raw food is risky" research are asking different questions. I look forward to the day when easily found studies that seek to balance the benefits and the risks clearly answer all questions. I encourage you to do your own research on the subject, talk it over with your veterinarian, and find a Therapy Dog organization to join that accommodates your beliefs and philosophy in diet.

The information in this chapter may feel overwhelming but I think of it as being like the rules for driving. There's a lot to learn and keep track of in the beginning but the more you do it the more automatic it becomes. The information in this chapter is what I'd teach any new Therapy Dog team I was mentoring. The difference is that when mentoring a new team I share these tips and guidance as

---

[22] By: Emily Vey - Reading Time: 7 minutes Updated On February 10, et al. "Raw Proof: New Research On Species-Appropriate Diets." *Dogs Naturally*, 10 Feb. 2020, www.dogsnaturallymagazine.com/new-research-on-species-appropriate-diets/.

circumstances dictate on visits and in this chapter I've tried to give it all to you at once.

Chapter Eight: Getting Started

Once you have a dog that you want to be a Therapy Dog and you've done the training work and taught the necessary skills, it's time to take the next step of joining a Therapy Dog organization. Why join an organization? There are three principal reasons for joining an organization: administrative support including volunteer liability insurance, credibility, and association. Let's look at each of these in turn.

Administrative Support

When you are part of a Therapy Dog organization you'll have a recognized non-profit behind you. The organization will maintain a website where facilities wanting visits can find out more information. They will also track health records of the dog, maintain Memorandums of Understanding (MOU), offer testing/evaluations, and provide you with credentials accrediting you as an approved Therapy Dog team.

You will pay annual dues/membership fees to any Therapy Dog organization you join. These membership fees/dues are used to pay for the administrative overhead including the organization's website, record keeping, and volunteer liability insurance.

Testing

A reputable organization will require an independent evaluation. Teams that have been independently evaluated against clearly defined standards have a lot more credibility. Chapter Five talked about the American Kennel Club (AKC) Canine Good Citizen (CGC) test and how the skills and behaviors needed to pass that test are a great foundation for passing Therapy Dog tests.

Therapy Dog tests are designed to test the dog's ability to remain calm and under control in the face of novelty and the unexpected. The tests will try to emulate some of the things that are likely to occur on a visit. As an evaluator for the organization I belong to, when I am evaluating a potential Therapy Dog team the first thing I look at is the dog's temperament. I want to see a dog that is calm and relaxed. I want to see a dog that is interested and engaged. And I want to see a dog that is under control, both self-control and control of the handler/partner.

The second thing I look for is connection. I want to see a potential team where each member is attentive to the other. A handler who is more interested in their phone than in their dog will raise some red flags, for example. If the dog is feeling nervous about things I want to see how the handler responds. Are they trying to soothe the dog or are they scolding the dog for not relaxing? How does the handler respond to the dog correctly performing a cue? Does the handler reinforce compliance or just assume it? I prefer to see reinforcement in the form of "good dog" and/or some petting. When a dog takes multiple tries to get a cue right, how does the handler react? I love to see handlers who try to figure out why the dog is having trouble and then find a way to remove or minimize that problem. Sometimes it's as simple as shifting position to block the dog's view of another dog they're concerned about.

As I watch for connection, I want to determine whether a dog is exhibiting stress because it's coming down the leash from the handler. The CGC separation exercise lets me see if the dog calms down when the handler's testing nerves are out of sight. Humans sometimes have an unreasonable fear of tests and the fact that they are going to be judged on how well they do scares them. Remember that in a Therapy Dog test, the worst possible outcome is that you don't pass and you come back and try again another time knowing which areas needed work in the meantime.

The final thing I look for is compliance. Does the dog respond correctly to cues? If the dog can't respond to a cue to stay, for example, I assume the potential team needs more training. I also look for whether the dog recognizes the cues. If the dog has no idea how to remain with the handler/partner when turning, I'll have some concerns about the communication between person and dog. And finally I am checking to see if the dog is listening to the handler. A dog that isn't listening in the novel and somewhat stressful environment of the test is going to have a very hard time listening on a visit.

When I tested with D'Artagnan we'd only been training together for about 10 weeks and I fully expected that we'd fail. I was hoping we'd pass but what I really expected was that we'd identify the things we'd need to work on for the next test. Instead, he did me proud and we passed with flying colors. My independent-minded dog who is entirely capable of blowing off any cue he doesn't feel like performing apparently understood that in these circumstances it was important to work with me and make me look good. We demonstrated that he is calm and relaxed in novel circumstances, that we have a strong connection, and that he understood and would comply correctly with cues. Despite the short period of training we were already a team.

Not all organizations have the same testing expectations. Some organizations require that you have completed training offered by them; others don't care where you trained or what your actual training was as long as you can meet their standards in testing. Some organizations use the language that you are a certified Therapy Dog team; others will say that you are registered. The difference between certified and registered often refers to where you received your training. If your training was provided by an organization, you will be certified while those who trained outside the organization's structure are registered. Either way you should have demonstrated suitability in a test, and an evaluator should have determined that you are indeed fit for the work.

Some organizations will test for suitability and then require a set number of supervised visits to confirm you and your dog can be a successful team. When this is done in a supportive manner you have the benefit of a one-on-one mentorship helping you to be the most successful team you can. However, there is the potential for the supervised visits to be highly stressful as you try to impress your accompanying evaluator. If you're the type that is more likely to feel judged than supported, an organization that doesn't require supervised visits is probably better suited to you. You are the best judge of what will suit you in an organization.

Arranging Visits: Memorandum of Understanding

Now that you've passed your test and registered with the organization, you choose what happens next. It is likely that you get to hurry up and wait. You'll wait for the organization to process your application and send your credentials. If the organization requires a handler's background check as well, the wait can be six weeks or more. But in time your credentials will arrive and you will be a fully accredited Therapy Dog team. Congratulations! Now what? If you're like most teams you'll be eager to get started and make your first official visit.

This is where a lot of new teams feel overwhelmed and confused. How do you find a place to visit? Who do you talk to? Are you supposed to just show up? These questions and more will often be running through the minds of new teams. Some organizations leave organizing their visits entirely in the hands of each individual team. Other organizations have group visits already in place that new teams are free to join. Organizations can emphasize one type of visiting, individual or group, over another or they will have both types of visiting available and new teams can choose which they prefer.

If you are arranging your own visits, you'll need to choose a facility you'd like to visit. Once you've selected a facility, check with your organization to see if there is an existing Memorandum of Understanding (MOU). MOUs spell out the responsibilities and expectations of each side. The specifics of what the

MOU says will vary from organization to organization but in general terms facilities can expect clean and professional teams to show up on time, to sign in, comply with facility rules, and for the dog to behave. Teams can expect facilities to provide someone to accompany them on visits, to be welcomed, and that the facility will not invite another organization's teams to visit at the same time. You can check whether an MOU exists between the organization and the facility in the members section of your organization's website or by emailing the organization and asking. When there is an MOU on file it's possible to schedule a visit. If there is not an MOU on file for a facility, you'll need to get a copy from your organization for the facility and have it signed and sent to the organization. It's a small bit of extra paperwork.

When you call the facility ask to speak to the Life Enrichment Coordinator or Activities Director. Let them know that you have a Therapy Dog with whom you would like to visit. You may need to explain what that means since there can be a lot of turnover in Life Enrichment staff. This is where a clear understanding of your organization's rules helps since you may need to explain how it works and what the

MOU is. Once you pass this hurdle, schedule and make your first visit. We'll talk about visits more in a later chapter.

Insurance

Reputable Therapy Dog organizations are nonprofit organizations and you will be a volunteer. As a volunteer the organization will carry liability insurance covering you should something unexpected happen on a visit and someone be harmed or expensive equipment damaged. Imagine you're visiting and your dog was sitting and getting petted by someone when someone else in a wheelchair accidentally ran over your dog's tail.[23] The sudden pain in the dog's tail caused the dog to leap up and accidentally knock into the person they'd been visiting who fell to the floor and broke their arm. In this imaginary scenario, it turns out to be a very complicated break requiring multiple surgeries to fix. If you are visiting without the protection of a Therapy Dog organization, whatever liability insurance you personally carry could be held responsible. If you have

---

[23] This possibility is why I highly encourage keeping track of your sitting dog's tail and gently tucking it around their paws.

no liability insurance you can be on the hook yourself. Facilities carry their own liability insurance and residents are covered by their personal coverage but no insurance will pay if they can shift the responsibility to someone else. Because the Therapy Dog organization carries liability insurance on you as a Therapy Dog team it will be up to the various insurance companies to sort out who pays what but should something happen if you are visiting under the auspices of a reputable organization, your personal insurance or finances won't be on the hook.

Credibility

When you're choosing which organization to join there are a number of factors to consider. The first thing to consider is where the organization is active in your area. There are two Therapy Dog organizations active where I live. Most of the Therapy Dog teams in my area belong to one of those two organizations. Consequently those are the organizations widely recognized among the facilities in the area. Someone from a different Therapy Dog organization asking to visit will have a harder time gaining permission to visit since their organization is not known; they'll be regarded as less credible.

Sometimes it can be uncomfortable to belong to one organization if the majority of teams in an area belong to another. In my experience teams from all the organizations active in my area respect and support one another, but that isn't necessarily true everywhere. Sometimes rivalries can develop making it harder for teams that don't belong to the dominant organization.

Organizations come in all shapes and sizes. Some of them will be active in a single city, state, or region. Others may be restricted to a single facility such as a hospital. There are also organizations that are active nationwide and even those that are international. A very local organization is likely to be tightly connected to its facilities and the teams are likely to be close friends. As you expand the coverage area of an organization it becomes more diffuse and less closely connected to the specific facilities it visits. Some of the teams may be virtual strangers. Some national and international organizations try to address this by creating local chapters, branches, or groups. In this model, teams visit together and form close lasting bonds with each other and with the facilities they visit.

When possible it's nice to meet handlers/partners that belong to the organization and talk to them. Personally, I really enjoyed hearing stories and advice from active teams when I first began. I learned a lot from them. You can also learn about an organization through online reviews and by visiting the organization's website.

How Many Species

The next question to consider about an organization is whether they are limited to canines or if they also approve other animals for Therapy work. There is a wide variety of choices about this. Some organizations limit membership to specific breeds, some organizations welcome dogs only, and some organizations evaluate and register Therapy Animal teams that can be cat, rabbit, goat, mini horse, horse, llama, and more. Many different animals can be very effective doing Therapy visits. Having more than merely dogs visit can be helpful to a facility. Some people have a fear of dogs but adore cats. and most people are thrilled by the novelty of a visit from a

Therapy Mini Horse so having a variety of Therapy Animals can make it easy to meet a variety of needs.

I like that so many different animals are available and tested for Therapy work. However, I recognize that the rules governing how a dog is equipped and handled on a visit and how a mini horse is equipped and handled aren't going to be the same. Dogs, for example, typically go barefoot but a mini horse needs rubber shoes so as not to damage floors. Dogs are a predator species and will react differently to certain stimuli than a prey species like a mini horse will. With a lot of different Therapy Animal rules, some of which apply to one species and not to others, some people might feel overwhelmed and confused about which rules apply to them and their dog. The organization I am a member of is limited to all breeds of dog. I find that, for me, that is the best choice. Your preference may be different.

Association

Another nice thing about belonging to an organization is that it gives you instant connection to other people who also want to work with their dogs to make the world a better place. Whether you are making Therapy Dog visits as an individual team or as part of a group of teams, the organization will enable you to easily find other friendly and generous people that love dogs. The immediate association you'll have with other Therapy Dog teams in your organization can lead to great friendships.

Both visiting with a group and visiting alone offer advantages and disadvantages. If you are visiting as an individual team, you can visit when it is convenient for you and easily change your visiting schedule as needed. That's not possible when multiple teams are visiting. As an individual, though, you will only be able to visit a few people. In a facility of 100 residents if you can only spend time visiting five or ten people that leaves a lot of disappointed people who didn't get to spend time with a dog. When a group of dogs visits, many more people get to spend time enjoying a dog's company. We'll talk more about visits in Chapter Ten.

It's a matter of personal preference whether you'd rather visit alone or as part of a group. Some people are happy to go it alone and others like to have support, especially when they're getting started. Some teams prefer to set their own visit schedule as time permits while others find it helpful to have regularly scheduled visits and built-in mentors. If you know whether group or individual visits are more appealing to you, check the preference of the organization you plan to join. If you prefer to go with others and the organization you plan to join does not support that, you might be better served by a different organization.

I hope this chapter has given you an idea of the benefits of joining a reputable Therapy Dog organization and an idea of what qualities you want to find in an organization. No organization is going to be perfect but you should be better able to decide which things are more important to you. When I started out I had no idea what to even consider about an organization. I just took the test for an organization I'd heard of when it was offered nearby and ended up getting lucky; it's been a good fit for me. The intent of this chapter is to give you tools to be better able to choose.

Chapter Ni

Facilities—Thi

Know

Every facility you visit will be different with its own quirks and peculiarities. In this chapter we'll explore the things I've learned that surprise people when they begin visiting. We'll talk about the varying quality of facilities and the unexpected considerations we need to keep in mind when visiting different places.

Facility Quality

Let's talk a bit about the types of facilities you'll be visiting and what to expect from them. New teams are often surprised at the wide range in quality between healthcare facilities. When visiting nursing homes, long-term care facilities, health and rehab facilities, and other convalescent centers you will discover that some places are delightful to visit where you would be happy to place your own parents and some facilities are less idyllic.

To comply with privacy rules we don't include faces of residents in our photos or we obscure the face before sharing them. Sometimes there is a moment that's so lovely you want to capture it for yourself. You'll never share it except with the person in the photo but you want to keep that moment fresh in memory forever.

One day we were visiting one of the less idyllic facilities and Ranger was immediately drawn to one of the residents. The two of them had such a happy Mutual Admiration Society going that I couldn't resist snapping a photo. I knew I wouldn't be able to share it anywhere but I wanted to capture that moment for myself. It was a lovely portrait and I emailed it to the facility so they could share it with the resident. Apparently the facility printed it out on a letter-sized sheet of paper. On our next visit the resident rushed back to their room to bring that picture to show us. It was a prized possession. That small act of kindness and the love of my dog brought a great deal of joy to someone. That's the power of Therapy Dog work.

Impact of Therapy Dog Visits

Everyone feels better when Therapy Dogs are around. I became aware of just how powerful Therapy

Dog visits are on a visit to one of the facilities Ranger and I visited with our group. The group was spread out up and down the hall visiting with people who'd come out of their rooms to see the dogs. I took a quick glance to check on the other teams and caught one handler/partner signaling me to come join them and the person they were talking to. When Ranger and I concluded our visit we strolled over. As I got close I could see the nametag the person was wearing read CEO. I joined them in time to hear him say how much the facility valued our visits and how much difference they made. As I thanked him for those kind words he added that the facility has a liberal pet visit policy so they get lots of dogs visiting. The dogs that are simply pets, however, would actually increase the stress in the facility while he could always tell when it was our trained Therapy Dogs visiting. "When you're visiting, the whole place feels happier and more relaxed." His office was on the top floor of the building and this was the first time I'd ever seen him so his testimonial that we made the entire facility feel happier and more relaxed was indeed praise.

When you think about it, though, it made sense. Your average pet is not used to going into strange and unfamiliar places with lots of peculiar things happening. Consequently that pet is going to be stressed and unsettled. And a stressed and unsettled pet is one that is inclined to act out and react badly to things they're finding frightening.

A pet visiting their person in a nursing home for the first time is almost the very definition of trigger stacking. The pet begins by being startled by the automatic door and before they've fully recovered from that, a large medicine cart rumbles down the hall straight at them. They are hit with a lot of unfamiliar chemical smells and hearing someone shouting at the other end of the hall. The floor they're walking on is very slippery so they're concentrating in order to not fall. Many different people rush by them, stopping to touch them without so much as a by your leave. Each one of those things adds a little bit to the dog's stress level until finally the dog has had enough and barks or snaps. In contrast those things are all in a day's work for a Therapy Dog. They start their visit with a lot more resilience than an average pet does, and they are partnered with and handled by someone who is more attuned to the dog's stress and is working hard to support the dog.

Therapy Dogs love their job but they also develop favorites, both favorite facilities and favorite people within facilities. I was always entertained by how Ranger could recognize the names of his favorite places. One day I made the mistake of telling Ranger we'd be going to one of his favorite facilities after he had his breakfast. As soon as Ranger heard the name he was at the gate whining to go. I ended up having to give him his breakfast in the car! There was no way he was going to miss out on a visit to a favorite place. Breakfast could wait.

Once we arrived at a facility Ranger would make his way first to the rooms of his favorite people. Over the years he learned that sometimes a favorite wouldn't be there anymore. On one visit we went to the room of a favorite to find it empty and awaiting a new occupant. Ranger sighed and we started visiting from room to room. When we knocked on the door of one room and were invited in, Ranger was beside himself with delight to find that his favorite had simply moved to a different room. For others that disappeared between one visit and the next, we seldom knew if they'd passed away, moved to a new facility, or gone home.

Safety and Hygiene

It's important to work with facilities to keep residents and patients safe. One way Therapy Dog teams can do this is to be very careful about bed and lap visits. First and foremost we need to abide by the rules of the facility we are visiting. Not all facilities have the same rules. The next thing is to be aware of the comfort of both the dog and the person being visited. For dogs doing a lap or bed visit, it's reassuring if their handler/partner keeps a hand on them and maintains physical contact with them. When a big dog is doing a 'paws up' on the edge of a bed, it's smart for the handler/partner to use their arm as an additional protective barrier so the dog doesn't accidentally bump the person being visited.

Many people in the older population have very fragile skin and even well trimmed and smoothed dog nails can rip that skin. So be sure to consider the safety of the person in the bed or chair that wants to hold the dog. In addition to protecting their fragile skin, we need to be aware that a person in a bed may have a wound, surgical incision, or other medical fragility that needs caution. Simply plopping a dog onto someone who wants to pet the dog risks causing them discomfort, pain, or further injury. Before placing a dog on someone's lap or into their bed, make sure it is okay with them and that there are no areas which should be avoided. If there are, do not allow the lap or bed visit. A dog merely shifting slightly to become more comfortable can tear fragile skin or exacerbate other issues. It is highly recommended that a dog doing a lap or bed visit be placed on a towel or something similar to protect fragile skin and reduce any spread of germs. Some organizations discourage bed and lap visits or prohibit them all together.

This brings us to the issue of hygiene. As a Therapy Dog team visiting a facility we are obligated to maintain good hygiene and do our part to prevent the spread of germs. Reputable Therapy Dog organizations have rules about how you conduct yourself on a visit and about the hygiene standards you should maintain. These rules include the expectations that your dog's paws never touch anything except the floor unless there is a protective barrier in place. Typically this barrier is a towel. You are expected to use a new towel in each room and in double rooms use a different towel for each bed.

If you visit hospitals you'll be expected to practice rigorous hygiene. Typically hospitals require volunteers to take additional training provided by the hospital. Few if any of them consider your organization's testing and evaluation sufficient to demonstrate suitability for hospital work. You and your dog will need to be cautious around a wide variety of medical equipment and extremely careful about tubes and wires. Whether you're visiting in patient rooms or just spending time comforting and supporting those in hospital waiting areas, stopping the spread of germs will be a very high priority. You'll need to make sure people sanitize their hands before and after petting your dog. You'll need to be fully acquainted with and compliant with hospital rules and protocols. This is another place that can be emotionally challenging for you and your dog since hospitals are literally places of life and death.

Schools and Libraries

Besides healthcare type facilities, you and your dog can listen to stories at schools and libraries. Schools can be very loud and chaotic between classes or when classes are released for recess. This can be hard on a dog's sensitive hearing and unsettling because of all the movement. Try to avoid being there at times when a lot of students will be in the hallways. In addition to the noise and chaos, masses of students may all want to pet your dog at once. This can be overwhelming for even the most stable and reliable dog. Consider that children are loud, unpredictable, and tend to move more erratically than adults. They also do not have the same personal space instincts as adults.

When Ranger and I had been volunteering at an afterschool program for about a year, we were invited to participate in an end-of-year assembly. We received the thanks and gratitude of the school for our volunteer work and I was asked to talk a little bit about dogs in general and Ranger in particular. After I spoke and Ranger showed off a few tricks, the assembled students applauded and cheered. Even though Ranger was well used to the noise of kids and was one of the most stable and reliable dogs I've ever known, that wave of applause echoing in the gym rocked him back a few steps. It was excessively loud to me and my hearing is nowhere near as acute as his was.

When visiting a school or library remember that some students and patrons will have allergies, which can sometimes be life-threatening. In addition to allergies to pet dander some people also have allergies to peanuts. These can be so life-threatening that it's recommended that we not give our dogs treats with peanut butter. We are obligated to do all we can to minimize the hazards to those we visit. Another way to help alleviate allergies is to keep your dog settled on their blanket to minimize the impact of pet dander.

Bear in mind that you may encounter students, staff, or library patrons who have a deep-seated fear of dogs. Your job is to respect that and give them the space they need to feel safe. Do not push them to overcome their fear or disregard it. You will do far more good respecting their fear than discounting it.

At one reading program Ranger and I participated in there was a student terrified of dogs. After weeks of us giving the student a wide berth and never intruding into their safe zone, the student asked to touch Ranger. I recognized the hesitation to approach him head on, so I had Ranger turn his back and I indicated a place on his lower back that could be touched. The student marveled at how soft he was. Over the course of several more weeks the student gradually reached a point where petting Ranger's neck was possible.

In schools and libraries you also interact with students who have no idea what appropriate behavior toward dogs is. You need to be constantly vigilant to protect your dog. If you are protecting your dog and heading off inappropriate behavior your dog will not have to take the matter into their own teeth. At libraries you'll often encounter babies and toddlers who are astonishingly fast and can have fingers in the dog's eyes, ears, or mouth in the blink of an eye. Or they can grab handfuls of fur and pull. This isn't much of an issue with a smooth coated dog but for rough coats this is a frequent hazard.

You are responsible to make sure that any problems or accidents are reported. On one hot day when we were visiting for a reading program, I gave Ranger a bowl of water on the corner of his blanket. He managed to knock it over. We mopped up all that we could but it did leave a damp spot on the rug under the blanket. We made sure to report that and explain that it was only water. We didn't want anyone to think that Ranger had had an accident.

In my experience libraries are good at making sure everyone on staff knows dogs will be coming for a reading program. The same is not always true of schools. Sometimes the teacher you're working with and the principal may be the only ones who know you'll be there. This can create situations where other teachers, custodial staff, or office staff may object to your presence and even try to prevent you from reaching the classroom where you will be volunteering. Be prepared to explain clearly and succinctly why you are there and where you are going. It also helps to be prepared with the phone number of the teacher and/or principal.

This chapter has highlighted some of the things to consider and be aware of about the different types of facilities you may visit as a Therapy Dog team. For the most part you will be welcomed with open arms and great delight. Everyone loves you and your Therapy Dog.

Chapter Ten: Visiting— What to Expect

Finally the day arrives when you will actually be making visits. This is the moment your training, practicing, and planning have been preparing you for. It's time for your Therapy Dog team to get to work.

No two visits will ever be the same, and the way things work will vary from place to place. There are, however, some general expectations and routines. When you arrive at the facility, unload your dog, give them a chance to take care of any business, walk them as necessary. Many dogs are more relaxed on a visit after a walk than if they arrive and go straight to work. My own dogs like to take a quick walk around the outside of the building—all the way around. When you enter the building expect to check in at reception. After checking in, wait for the Life Enrichment staff member that will be taking you around. If you're very familiar with the facility, their routine, expectations, and rules, you might be free to decide where you're going to visit and head out on your own. Broadly speaking, there are two types of visits. One is that you and your dog will go from room to room visiting with the residents in their rooms. The other type has residents assembled in big groups and you will go from person to person around the circle.

With experience a Therapy Dog will become very adept at figuring out how best to engage with the person they are visiting. As the handler/partner our job is to support the dog and not micromanage the dog's interaction. A Therapy Dog should never be forced to engage with someone they do not choose. I like to remind myself that my dog has far more acute senses than I do. If my dog says he'd rather not visit someone I respect that he has his reasons. The converse is true as well. If my dog says it's important to visit someone I believe him.

Visiting Alone Versus Visiting as Part of a Group

I've done both individual visits and group visits and I personally prefer to visit with a group. When you visit in a group many more people get to spend time with a dog. You're also able to pick and choose which team visits which resident. When I walk into a room with my giant dog and discover that the resident had small dogs all their life and prefers them, I can find a team with a small dog in my group to visit them. Or if a resident has a long history with a particular breed, a team with that breed in the group could visit that resident.

In doing group visits we also discovered that the dogs will often specialize. Most dogs prefer to avoid tight smothery hugs and loud people with big uncontrolled movements but for one of the dogs in our group, those are his people. When we meet someone who wants to squeeze the dogs or a bigger-than-life person or someone who has really big movements, we make sure they get to visit with Wilson. Meanwhile, Harry has made it his mission to make sure staff get the benefits of Therapy Dog time when they need it. He has a real genius for sniffing out the staff members that are having a particularly hard day and zeroing in on them to make sure they get some love and attention. We all encourage staff to spend a bit of time with the dogs but we've learned that if Harry has targeted a particular staff member, the rest of us should make sure to give that person some extra attention too.

When they visit as part of a group the dogs learn to know each other in the group and to work together as colleagues and friends. Many times on group visits we would run into someone's pet who took exception to our visiting dogs. Often I'd see the dogs looking out for each other: a bigger dog would move to screen a smaller dog, a dog with excellent social skills would distract the pet, or many other examples of canine communication would occur.

On one visit we were walking down the hall to another section of the facility when we met someone carrying their newly adopted Chihuahua mix. The Chihuahua freaked out at meeting other dogs in the hallway and screamed and struggled to get down, apparently with the intent of attacking the other dogs. In order to keep all the dogs safe and allow the upset little dog as much room to pass as possible, all the teams headed to the wall on the far side of the hall. The handlers/partners weren't paying much attention to how the dogs were arranging themselves along the wall since they could feel how calm their own dog was through the leash. When I looked I noticed that our dogs had arranged themselves so that there was the least chance of any of them getting injured and the most chance that conflict could be avoided. The two largest and calmest dogs were in the front, the medium sized dog was in the middle and the two smallest ones were behind him. If the Chihuahua had attacked, the big dogs in front were both very good at defusing situations so could probably take care of any potential conflict. If the Chihuahua had somehow gotten past the big dogs, he would have run into the Flat-Coated Retriever who was large enough not to be threatened by the Chihuahua. The most vulnerable dogs who actually could have been hurt in a fight with the Chihuahua were well protected.

Visits can also be challenging for humans. If you visit as part of a group sometimes you'll see another human becoming overwhelmed. You can pull them aside for a quick word or just lend your support as needed. When you visit as a group, there is time after the visit to stand in the parking lot and debrief, decompress, and download your experiences with people who know exactly what you're talking about. Individual visits don't have that after-visit support.

Visiting

School Versus Library

If your dog is one that listens to kids read you'll find yourself at a school or a library. These are actually very different from each other. Some dogs are comfortable at either, but other dogs will prefer one type of reading venue over the other. In a library readers will be all ages from toddlers to teens. Libraries also have a lot more movement and noises than a school. Some dogs find the busyness of a library overstimulating or overwhelming.

In a school setting dogs are typically visiting only one classroom so the students are all comparable in age and size. Because the other students are doing schoolwork quietly at their desks while specific students are having their turn to read to the dog, school settings are very quiet and calm. Nothing much is happening so the dog can relax. However, some dogs find the enforced quiet oppressive and with nothing to watch except the pages of a book being slowly turned, they can become bored. When that happens the dog can get restless and may act up. Other dogs will enjoy the peace and quiet and have a nap. Your dog will tell you whether they prefer schools or libraries or have no preference. It's up to us to listen.

When visiting a school or library, take a blanket or mat for your dog to lie on. It's a good idea if you've practiced a 'place' cue with your dog using that blanket or mat. Dogs don't usually generalize very well so if the first time they see the blanket or mat is at the school or library, they may be reluctant to use it. Because I have big dogs I have a lightweight blanket that is big enough for both dog and reader to be on it together.

Colleges and Universities

An incredibly fun and rewarding place to visit can be college and university campuses doing stress relief before midterms or finals. Students are thrilled to see the dogs and pet them. Many of them are missing their own dog at home and looking forward to seeing them again. It can be overwhelming for some dogs to have a crowd of adult- sized kids all petting them at once, but if your dog enjoys it, a campus visit is like a trip to the best massage parlor in the world. Ranger loved it. If someone stopped petting him,

Ranger would reach out with his great big paw and tap the person, which always earned him a big laugh and instant compliance. His message was clear, "Don't stop; get back to the petting." I remember one student settling on the ground at Ranger's head and petting him with great attention and concentration before popping back to their feet and announcing, "There, I'm ready for my final!"

Surprises on Visits

You never know what to expect on a Therapy Dog visit. On one memorable visit to a memory care facility, we entered and all the dogs made a beeline for a particular resident. We hadn't seen this resident before, but the dogs always seem to recognize the dog people on sight so we didn't think much of it until the person reached down in the wheelchair and pulled out a napkin full of bacon. When this person heard the dogs would be there, they prepared by collecting all the bacon from breakfast they could. No wonder the dogs were so excited; put on enough bacon perfume and no dog can resist you. Of course it was left to the handlers/partners to explain to the person and the dogs why the dogs couldn't have all the bacon. We compromised by giving the dogs miniscule bits of bacon for doing tricks.

On a visit where everyone was together in a big room, our visit overlapped with a musician who was volunteering his time to sing and play for the residents. He was choosing songs that would be familiar to the residents and decided that with the dogs visiting he should perform every song he could think of that had anything to do with dogs. He was singing the Elvis Presley classic "You Ain't Nothin' but a Hound Dog" when suddenly Ranger decided to add some percussive barking. He threw in three or four barks on the beat. Everyone found this highly entertaining. The musician began adding his own barks to the lyrics, which got the residents adding their own barks as well. Ranger listened to all the barking for a bit, apparently well satisfied with what he'd started, then suggested it was time to leave and do some room visits.

Memory Care Units

Memory care facilities can be particularly challenging. There is something deeply unsettling in spending time with people who are untethered from the common timeline. This can be hard for some handlers/partners and occasionally for a dog. Most dogs don't seem to mind Memory Care units but some do not find it comfortable to visit there. Ranger loved visiting Memory Care facilities. I think he knew it was a place where he could do incredible good. A dog has a way of anchoring a person in the now without worrying about where else their mind might be traveling. It can make a huge difference for Memory Care patients to spend time with a dog.

Because Memory Care units typically house the ambulatory confused, these units are locked for the safety of the residents. Locked doors prevent them from wandering away and getting lost or hurt. The units are accessed by keycode. Some of the facilities we visited had these codes printed in a cryptic fashion while for others the code was only accessible to staff. In the latter staff would let you in and out.

Hospice

I've never personally made visits to hospice facilities but from time to time at our regular facility visits, we get asked to make hospice visits. These can be emotionally hard while being especially rewarding.

When my group has been asked to make hospice visits, some teams know they'll have a hard time dealing with it and decline. Those that are comfortable with it will go in one at a time with their dog. If the person is alone we try to engage them with the dog and feel well rewarded if we earn a smile or the dog gets a pat. We understand that we're visiting someone very close to the end of life and have given them a moment of pleasure, however brief.

When visiting one facility with Ranger I experienced just how precious those end-of-life smiles are. I still remember that particular visit. The activities director was taking us around and telling my group which residents needed a visit. As she directed me into one room she told me the resident was near the end of life and might not be responsive. I remember thinking, "Gee, thanks a lot." Ranger and I went in and I asked him to walk up beside the bed while I told the resident that Ranger had come to visit. A hand reached vaguely toward the side of the bed and Ranger pushed his head under it then shifted until the hand was resting on his back. A small smile appeared on the face of the resident and they stayed like that for several minutes until the hand retreated back into the bed and Ranger led me out of the room. That little smile is the reason Therapy Dog teams do what we do.

When family members are with the hospice patient, we visit briefly with the patient and then the dogs go to work on the family getting them to pet them and engage with them. Sometimes the dogs will choose to be silly, which will get a laugh. It feels like the dogs are trying to remind the family that despite their impending loss, life will go on and there will still be happiness to be found. If you're visiting a hospice facility you may visit the same patient and their family several times before the end, or between one visit and the next the person may be gone. It isn't easy work but for those who feel drawn to hospice work, it is incredibly fulfilling.

Atypical Visiting

Pandemic lockdown and the attendant social isolation were hard on everyone but especially so for those in care facilities. The local Therapy Dog group that I manage has built close relationships with the facilities we visit, and we wanted to find ways we could still lift their spirits even when we couldn't visit in person. In order to maintain our connection and find ways for the residents to still enjoy the dogs, we had to think outside the box.

The first thing we did was relatively simple. Each week we sent a new photo of our dogs to the Life Enrichment Coordinator who printed them out and posted them around the facility. I included a short note with D'Artagnan's photo written as if D'Artagnan was the author. This grew into a new weekly Facebook Album where all the photos are gathered. Each week had a different theme. This Facebook album allowed us to reach more facilities since they could see the Facebook pages without having to print multiple pictures every week.

As the pandemic wore on, D'Artagnan and I experimented with virtual visits. The plan was that D'Artagnan and I would test it out with one of our facilities. If it worked out well we'd add more people and make it a regular event. Virtual visits are a lot different than visiting in person. Because my laptop doesn't have a working webcam, I used a standalone webcam. D'Artagnan doesn't notice the built-in webcam that blends into the case of the laptop but he definitely noticed the single big eye—that's how he perceives it—staring at him continually. Staring is extremely rude in dog society and can be an act of aggression. Consequently, as the virtual visit went on, D'Artagnan got progressively less comfortable. We also struggled with the technical challenges of getting him to stay where he and I could both be seen. If I was back far enough to have D'Artagnan and myself both visible, the microphone had trouble picking my voice up. It was an interesting challenge and that first virtual visit was not a rousing success.

I solved the technical issues by adding a second laptop with a working webcam so we could have the freestanding webcam focused at me and the built-in webcam focused on D'Artagnan. I added Bluetooth headphones and microphone so everyone could hear each other. Things were better but in the end we abandoned the experiment as simply too complicated. I've heard that other teams have managed it successfully but it didn't work out for us.

During the summer when some of the lockdown restrictions eased, we did performance visits. Several teams appropriately masked and distanced from one another would walk around the outside of the building and do tricks for small groups of residents who were arranged widely spaced in several different areas outside. This proved to be a lot of fun for residents and dogs alike, although the dogs were confused about why they couldn't go and solicit petting as usual. The downside of these visits is that they require good weather.

This led us to explore video as a means of maintaining our connection and letting the residents see the dogs. We started our own YouTube channel and posted some short videos of our dogs. The downside was that many of the handlers/partners aren't sufficiently tech savvy to be able to do this and so not many videos are available.

I hope this chapter has given you some idea about the general structure of visits and some of the different ways you can visit without being present in person. Visits are incredibly rewarding and delightfully unpredictable. They are at the core of what we do.

Conclusion

It is my deep hope that in these pages many of your questions were answered and you now feel confident and empowered to embark on your journey to become a Therapy Dog team. I mentor a lot of teams in person. This book's goal was to capture those lessons in written form to help those interested in the work learn what it's like and how to get started. I've been engaged in Therapy Dog work for over a decade and have learned a lot along the way. In these pages I've shared with you the lessons I've learned and the things I wish I'd known when I began this journey. It has been a labor of love.

Whether you read this book because you were simply curious about Therapy Dog work or because you wanted to get started as a Therapy Dog team, I trust you found what you were looking for and that the guidance and advice I've shared in these pages has satisfied your curiosity and inspired you to take the next steps in becoming a Therapy Dog Team.

Therapy Dog work is fascinating, challenging, rewarding, and filled with the unexpected. I've tried to provide an honest description of what it's like.

Although the work isn't always easy, the impact a Therapy Dog team has is mind-blowing. Even when it is fraught with challenges, the incredible difference you can make as a Therapy Dog team makes it all worth it. I once jokingly remarked to an Activities Director that our dogs brought magic with them. He looked at me with all seriousness and replied, "They really do!" In the years I've been doing Therapy Dog work I've seen time and time again that miracles and magic do follow in the wake of a Therapy Dog team and it's nothing less than extraordinary.

As Therapy Dog teams we give generously from the heart. You might say we are unsung heroes quietly going about the business of helping people feel less alone, comforting those dealing with traumas, supporting those who are frightened, and encouraging those that need a boost to their confidence. Whether a Therapy Dog team visits people in a hospital, nursing home, memory care unit, library, courthouse, or disaster site, we bring healing and connection. Therapy Dog teams make the world a better place. By visiting those who are lonely and feel forgotten, we enrich their lives and give them something to look forward to.

In these pages I've explained what it takes to become a Therapy Dog team and we've delved into the mechanics. We've explored what a Therapy Dog is both in the legal and the abstract sense. You've learned the specialized roles Therapy Dogs can fill as well as their usual role of visiting. Although it's pretty straightforward to add listening to stories to a Therapy Dog's visits, you now understand that working at crisis and disaster sites or in a courthouse will require additional training and study. If you feel drawn to court or crisis work, you should be better equipped to understand and seek out the additional training you need. You should also have an idea of what an incredible gift it is to share your dog in these situations. Teams that do this kind of work are beyond price.

A lot goes into the making of a Therapy Dog. Discovering that you and your dog have the qualities needed to succeed in the job opens the door to a world of opportunities to make a difference. Together with your calm, attention-loving dog that genuinely loves all people you will comfort the lonely, calm the distressed, and bring laughter and love to all sorts of people.

By building a strong foundation for resilience and teaching your dog good manners, you've helped your dog manage the stresses of Therapy Dog work. The descriptions and explanations in these pages have also shown you how to recognize when that resilience is being depleted and stress is creeping in. Being aware of how our dogs are feeling makes us better handlers/partners, which helps us be more effective Therapy Dog teams.

I hope this book has taught you that there is far more to Therapy Dog work than simply walking around letting people pet your dog. Therapy Dog work is really a way to make the world a little bit better, make the lives of those you visit a little brighter, and be a force for good. Through Therapy Dog work we impact people's emotions in a positive way helping those that are unhappy, lonely, confused, or dejected feel better. Therapy Dog work is something you and your dog do together. It isn't something that you do and your dog just comes along. Nor is it something you transport your dog to so the dog can do everything. Therapy Dog work is truly a collaboration and together you are a team. It affords the chance for you and your dog to work as a unit and become even closer and more bonded.

Joining a Therapy Dog organization is the gateway to doing Therapy Dog work; belonging to one provides many benefits. Administrative support is, of course, one of the most valuable benefits. However, there is great value to the name recognition and positive reputation that comes from association with an organization as well. In many ways the greatest value is found in the mentors and friends that you gain through membership. In a world where making new friends can sometimes be challenging, Therapy Dog work connects you to others that share a passion for dogs and making the world better. It's a special kind of connection.

No matter where you visit you'll make an immense difference in the lives of the people you see. For many of these people a visit from a Therapy Dog team will be the highlight of their month. The time you take to really see and connect with the people you visit is a tremendous gift. When we, like our dogs, can learn to not be concerned with a person's appearance, condition, or mental acuity and instead can simply accept people and appreciate them, we become the best Therapy Dog team we can.

Thank you for reading this book and for being a person who wants to help. I hope that I've given you the knowledge and skills needed to become a Therapy Dog team. As you put what you've learned into practice I hope my advice and experience guide you on your way. The world needs more people who care about others and want to make things better. You're an amazing person with an incredible dog and together you'll be able to do astonishing things. Thank you for becoming a Therapy Dog team.

Acknowledgments

This book comes with unbounded gratitude for my sister Karla Sigrist for her exceptional skills as an editor. The book would be far less readable without her expertise. I have unbounded gratitude also for my husband Douglas Winder, son David Winder, and especially for my daughter Alexandra Winder. They've put up with my demands for countless readings and discussions of the manuscript, proofreading, general encouragement, technical support, hand-holding, and endless cups of tea. Truly, I could not have done this without them.

Special thanks go to Christy Gordon for her skill at transforming my rough mock-up into an attractive and enticing book cover. She does beautiful work.

Thanks also to Canine Principles Skills Hub for offering the course that spawned this book and to all the amazing people in the book group on Facebook. Their encouragement held me up when the doubts came.

Special thanks and gratitude go out to the wonderful handler/partners and their incredible dogs in my Therapy Dog group. They are my inspiration. Watching them in action is a constant source of joy both to me and to those they visit.

Last but by no means least, my heartfelt gratitude goes to Ranger who introduced me to Therapy Dog work and brought so much joy to so many people. Someday we'll meet again on the other side of the Rainbow Bridge. And to D'Artagnan who keeps me engaged in Therapy Dog work helping me to learn new ways to bring people joy and never passes up the opportunity to engage with another person.

Author Bio

When Dr. Katha Miller-Winder was working on completing her doctoral degree she expected to end up as a professor teaching Political Science somewhere. But life had different plans and by the time she'd successfully defended her dissertation she'd outgrown those early expectations. After a cancer diagnosis and treatment she adopted a dog and the rest, as they say, is history.

She's been a Therapy Dog handler/partner for a decade now. She serves as the director for a local group that's part of a well respected Therapy Dog organization and recently became an evaluator for the organization. She has encouraged, supported, observed, and mentored a lot of Therapy Dog teams over the years. When she has a passion for something Dr. Miller-Winder throws herself into it and learns everything she can about the subject. Dogs, especially Therapy Dogs and Therapy Dog work, are no exception. In order to be the best possible partner for her Therapy Dogs she's studied and researched canine body language, dog behaviorism, and current scientific research on dog behavior and training.

Dr. Miller-Winder lives in the Pacific Northwest where she shares her life with a beloved husband, grown children, assorted cats, some pond fish, and her current Therapy Dog, D'Artagnan, a Great Pyrenees. D'Artagnan is the successor to Katha's first dog Ranger who led her into Therapy Dog work.

As Dr. Miller-Winder puts it, "While working with Therapy Dogs I've seen amazing things happen, learned a lot, and along the way we've made the world a little better place by bringing company, laughter, and love to those who most need it. No one likes to feel forgotten and alone; with Therapy Dogs on the job they don't have to."

Connect with the Author

I hope you've enjoyed the book and that it has answered your questions. If you'd like to stay in touch you can follow Dr. Miller-Winder on social media:
Facebook: Becoming a Therapy Dog Team
TikTok: TherapyDogHandler
Email: DrKathaMillerWinderauthor@gmail.com

Works Cited

"ADA Requirements Service Animals." *ADA 2010 Revised Requirements: Service Animals*, U.S. Department of Justice Civil Rights Division Disability Rights Section, 24 Feb. 2020. www.ada.gov/service_animals_2010.htm.

American Kennel Club. "An Owner's Manual for: by the American Kennel Club 10 Essential Skills: CGC Test Items." *AKC.org*, images.akc.org/pdf/ebook/CGC2.pdf.

"Animal-Assisted Therapy Research." *UCLA People-Animal Connection*, www.uclahealth.org/pac/animal-assisted-therapy.

"Animals in Court and Related Settings - Welcome to Animals & Society Institute: Ann Arbor Michigan." *Welcome to Animals & Society Institute | Ann Arbor Michigan*, Animals & Society Institute, 28 Nov. 2018. www.animalsandsociety.org/helping-animals-and-people/for-judges-prosecutors-and-criminal-justice-professionals/resources-for-professionals-interested-in-including-animals-in-court-and-related-settings.

Emily Vey "Raw Proof: New Research On Species-Appropriate Diets." *Dogs Naturally*, 10 Feb. 2020, www.dogsnaturallymagazine.com/new-research-on-species-appropriate-diets/.

"Courthouse Facility Dog." *Wikipedia*, Wikimedia Foundation, 30 Dec. 2020, en.wikipedia.org/wiki/Courthouse_facility _dog.

"Definition of a Service Dog vs. Emotional Support Animal vs. Therapy Dog." *American Humane*, American Humane First to Serve, www.americanhumane.org/app/uploads/2 018/05/Definition-of-Service-Dog_3_7_18.compressed.pdf.

Rebecca F. Wisch. "FAQs on Emotional Support Animals." *Animal Law Legal Center*, 2015, www.animallaw.info/article/faqs-emotional-support-animals.

"Full Page Reload." *IEEE Spectrum: Technology, Engineering, and Science News*, spectrum.ieee.org/automaton/robotics/hu manoids/what-is-the-uncanny-valley.

Geier, Elisabeth. "The Astounding Heroics of Disaster Relief Dogs." *The Dog People by Rover.com*, 8 June 2018, www.rover.com/blog/service-dogs-disaster-relief.

Jones, Jacqueline. "Perceptions of the Impact of Pet Therapy on Residents/Patients and Staff in Facilities Visited by Therapy Dogs." *Therapy Dogs International*, https://www.tdi-dog.org/About.aspx?Page=Media+Kit.

"Oklahoma City Bombing, April 1995 Heartache in the Heartland." *Therapy Dogs International*, Therapy Dogs International, https://www.tdi-dog.org/OurPrograms.aspx?Page=DSRD+(Disaster+Stress+Relief+Dogs).

Ramirez, Ken, and Nini Bloch. *The Eye of the Trainer: Animal Training, Transformation, and Trust.* Karen Pryor Clicker Training, a Subsidiary of Sunshine Books, 2020.

"Raw Pet Foods and the AVMA's Policy: FAQ." *American Veterinary Medical Association*, www.avma.org/raw-pet-foods-and-avmas-policy-faq.

"Reading to Dogs: A Library's Guide to Getting Started." *Research - Reading to Dogs: A Library's Guide to Getting Started*, readingtodogs.weebly.com/research.html.

Schneider, Susan M. *The Science of Consequences: How They Affect Genes, Change the Brain, and Impact Our World.* Prometheus Books, 2012.

"Service Animals." *ADA 2010 Revised Requirements: Service Animals*, www.ada.gov/service_animals_2010.htm

"Statutes, Codes, and Regulations." *Legal Research Tools from Casetext*, www.casetext.com/statute/code-of-alabama/title-12-courts/chapter-21-evidence-and-witnesses/article-1-general-provisions/division-2-witnesses/subdivision-1-generally/section-12-21-147-use-of-registered-therapy-dog-in-certain-legal-proceedings.

Therapy Dogs International. *Therapy Dogs International (TDI) Testing Requirements*. tdi-dog.org.

"What Is AAT/AAA?" *Therapy Animals*, www.animaltherapy.net/what-is-aataaa/.

"What Is Animal Assisted Activities & Therapy (AAA/T)?" *Therapy Dogs Ohio | Animal Assisted Therapy Columbus Ohio | Angel Paws*, angelpawstherapy.org/what-is-animal-assisted-activities--therapy-aaat.html.

Index

Printed in Great Britain
by Amazon